THE BLOOMING LAWN

The Blooming Lawn

Creating a Flower Meadow

YVETTE VERNER

Illustrated
by Susan R. Davies

CHELSEA GREEN PUBLISHING COMPANY
White River Junction, Vermont

First published in the USA in 1998
by Chelsea Green Publishing Company
Post Office Box 428
White River Junction, Vermont 05001

Cover design by Rick Lawrence

Typeset in Sabon at Green Books
Totnes, Devon, England

Printed web offset by Biddles Ltd, Guildford, UK
Text paper: Five Seasons 100% recycled, acid-free

Library of Congress Cataloguing-in-Publication data
Verner, Yvette, 1947-
[Creating a flower meadow]
The blooming lawn : creating a flower meadow / Yvette Verner.
p. cm.
Includes bibliographical references (p.   ) and index.
ISBN 1-890132-18-7 (paperback)
1. Meadow ecology. 2. Gardening to attract wildlife. I. Title.
QH541.5.M4V47 1998   577.4'6--dc21
98-3944   CIP

Contents

Acknowledgements

The publishers would like to thank Ben Watson for providing details of North American species; David Westbrook of Somerset Wildlife Trust for advice on native British trees; David Fee of Devon Wildlife Trust for advice on butterflies; and Nicky Scott and Nicola Stanbury for advice on the ecological aspects of flower meadows.

Foreword

by David Bellamy

When people first turned up in force in sunny Sussex by the sea, the English landscape was covered with forest alder and willow in the valley bottoms, with a mixture of oak, elm, ash, hazel and a few others on the better-drained slopes. Travel was a slow and painful process; open spaces and far distant views were very rare unless you stood on the coast. In truth, you couldn't see the landscape for the trees. Ancient, natural woodland—it was full of wonderful plants and animals that had made it to Sussex before the meltwaters of the last Ice Age had refilled the English Channel, cutting us off from Europe.

In terms of biodiversity—that buzz word of the 1990s—well, it wasn't that great. On cliff tops, rocky outcrops and banks eroded by the river there were open communities and wetlands where spring flowers could bloom and butterflies, crickets and all the other creepy-crawlies that don't like too much shade could sing their songs and display their wings.

The first farmers changed all that: first using polished stone, then axes of bronze and iron, they cleared the forest for protection from attack, to graze their animals and eventually to plant their crops. So it was that the Sussex landscapes that I cycled through as a little boy came into existence: a rural landscape of hedgerows, coppice woodlands, fallow fields, pastures and of course meadows, people-made and people-managed, bursting with biodiversity.

Sadly, so much of that has changed in my lifetime with the march of changing farm practice and the commuter lifestyles that have gone with it. In places, the biodiversity of our countryside is at an all-time low.

This is a wonderful book that shows how each and every one of us can change all that, if only we care enough. Yvette and Mike did just that. They cared enough to spend their hard-earned wages, not on re-decorating the house or a new car, but on buying a tiny piece of land and putting it back into working order as a living, breathing meadow, giving them and their lucky neighbours an ever-changing panoply of nature, season by season.

That is all I need say. It is an inspiring story of our times, but it is much more than that for it is a *vade mecum* of how it was done and how you—yes you, the reader—can do it for yourself.

Bedburn
April 1998

Introduction

The environment affects us all, but how to translate such famous sayings as "think globally, act locally" and "small is beautiful" into personal actions is not always immediately apparent. This book is the result of a desire to give nature a helping hand in a personal way, with the added benefit that the results are easily visible. National and international organisations are vital in the struggle to protect our environment and halt the decline in biodiversity, but this book aims to show how we ordinary people can also help directly.

Flowering hay-meadows, prairies, savannah and tundra are fast disappearing the world over, but most homes are accompanied by a garden—be it large or small. An instinctive appreciation of flowers and grasses has resulted in the creation of millions of these carefully tended plots of land.

Despite our love of flowers, many gardens are mostly laid to lawn, which contributes little to maintaining species diversity—indeed, lawns are little more than 'green deserts'. Instead, why not have waving meadow grasses, with a succession of colourful wild flowers? Simple winding mown paths through your garden meadow will enable you to relax in a deckchair amongst butterflies and blossom, lulled to sleep by the humming of bees rather than woken by the buzzing of a hover-mower.

True enough, come July, it will be time to cut your mini-meadow, but a yearly bout of the bygone activity of haymaking will return your lawn to normal use until the autumn. In so doing, a multitude of native creatures, both beautiful and mysterious, will have benefited by your actions, and a tiny patch of the world will be living in tune with itself.

Before we bought our little meadow, we practised in our garden, which is only ten yards square. Just by leaving the mower in the shed we discovered a multitude of wild flowers which had evidently been waiting years for the opportunity to grow tall and bloom amongst the grass. To these we added chosen plants from a wild flower nursery, and before we realized it a mini-meadow was born.

We found that meadow creation is both absorbing and relaxing— a wonderful combination! Although it is not as instant as stocking up with bedding plants on a Saturday and having neat bands of colourful flowers by Sunday, the end result is well worthwhile, improving and evolving each year. The thrill of seeing your first wild primrose bud open, spotting a plump vole pausing to groom, or watching a swallow swoop down to snap up a gnat hovering above grass rippling in the breeze, is ample reward for any initial period when little appears to be growing. And poor soil is no handicap— indeed it is often particularly suitable for growing meadow species.

When we first bought our plot of land, we hoped we were doing our bit for the environment, imagining that, with our busy lives, we would occasionally look in to check how things were growing. We did not anticipate the pleasure a meadow brings. We had no idea how refreshing and therapeutic it would be to stroll round and simply watch the grass grow, see the flowers emerge and later admire the kaleidoscope of autumn leaves.

Our little meadow is now seven years old, and has held many surprises. Different flowers predominate each year, butterfly and insect populations flourish, with bird and animal life increasing as a result. A family of six badgers visited one year, with much good-humoured pushing and shoving and general play that was a delight to watch. Our trees and hedges have mostly overcome their initial hesitation and are growing fast. Together, these interdependent species have produced a meadow that is a living, breathing entity. Wherever it is situated, your meadow too will possess an air of tranquillity. Try it and see.

Yvette Verner
April 1998

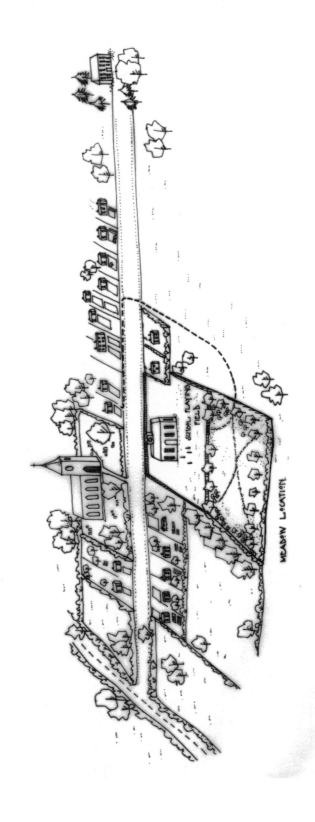

❧ Chapter 1 ❧

Finding Our Meadow

UNDER A CLEAR blue sky, a line of mature trees marks the far boundary of a small meadow. Thick hedges enclose the three remaining sides, and tall grasses ripple in the light summer breeze. Gleaming buttercups and daisies seem to float on this central green lagoon, while smaller flowers in shades of red, cream and mauve are glimpsed swimming in the depths beneath.

A cuckoo calls as I lean on the five-bar gate... and fall over. My vision of a flowery meadow disintegrates along with the woodwork, for as yet they do not exist other than in my imagination. Instead, I gaze at the not unpleasing—but nonetheless daunting—reality of an undulating grassy field, with just the far line of sturdy oaks and field maples to give substance to my dream. Practical but unpoetic barbed wire fences straddle the Northern and Southern edges, while the nearest (Western) side remains open to the larger field which adjoins it. Dreams are great in theory, but inevitably require a good deal of hard work to become reality. "So how," I asked myself, "had it all begun?"...

"This may be a silly idea," Mike said, as we pondered whether or not we could gather together enough money to re-tile the roof of our tiny cottage, "but why don't we buy a small piece of land for a nature reserve instead?"

Such a leap of lateral thinking attracted me immediately. Never mind the practicalities, like where would we find any land, or how could we afford it, or even what we should do about the roof!

Enticing vistas of sunlit wooded glades and sweeping hillsides beck-
oned. "Good idea—why not?"

Over the next year we advertised in local newspapers and left
our requirements with bewildered estate agents, who were more
used to dealing with requests for entire farms than for an odd piece
of land. We tried to be realistic: any scrubby corner of unwanted
ground would do, but we soon discovered that nobody parts with
land easily.

It was just after Christmas 1991 that an unexpected opportunity
arose. The landowners at the top of our lane were moving, so I wrote
to ask if they would consider selling us a small piece of land for a
wildlife sanctuary. Luckily, the eccentricity of this request appealed
to them, and some time later I met Mrs. Heatherley out walking her
dogs. "There is a piece of land you might be interested in," she
smiled. "Would you like to see it?"

Ten minutes later we were standing in the centre of an L-shaped
field, which enfolded two sides of the local village primary school.
January sunshine filtered weakly down from an overcast sky. The
trees were mere skeletons and pale grass squelched underfoot, but it
was land, real land, and a part of it was on offer to us. With no doubt
unseemly haste I said "We'd love it", and the legal wheels began to
turn. As spring merged into summer, the land was still tantalizingly
just out of reach; but one Saturday morning in July, thanks to the
kindness and empathy of the original landowners, we were able to
stand and gaze at our very own ground—albeit only half an acre!

How you picture half an acre depends on your point of view.
Farmers could no doubt blink and miss it whilst counting their cows
in for milking, or separating their sheep from their goats. Plenty of
people have half-acre gardens, neatly laid to lawn and flower beds.
On the other hand, our cottage garden is three yards square, so to
be suddenly confronted with an area some 40 yards by 50 yards was
a heady experience. The question of what to do with it had been
occupying my mind since that first tempting New Year glimpse. The
'scrubby corner' which had initially seemed the most likely outcome
of our search, would probably have been relatively easy to maintain. However, to be presented with a corner of what had once been
a hay meadow, even though not an ancient one, was a different
proposition entirely.

The disappearance of over ninety-five per cent of our flowering meadows during the last fifty years is so well documented that our desire to try and preserve a tiny fragment for the future seemed almost automatic. I say 'almost' because meadows are, of course, a man-made feature, and as such require managing. Easy enough for a farmer to drive his tractor around a field, cutting swathes of grass to be tidily baled and collected later; and even a large suburban lawn can be kept neatly shaved by regular Sunday afternoon mowings. Yet for an ordinary family, dealing with even a small field of hay promised to be somewhat challenging. An overall management plan was obviously called for, and one did indeed evolve, after much scribbling on scraps of paper, screwing them up and starting again.

The first necessity, however, was to fence off our portion of the field, as grazing cattle are no respecters of invisible demarcation lines. Accordingly a sturdy post and rail fence of oak and chestnut was ordered, together with a traditional five-bar gate (primarily for leaning upon and gazing across purposes). A second smaller gate was also required where our Right of Way through the larger section of the field met the lane, so a brief description of exactly how our little field is situated may be useful at this point.

Like many villages these days, ours is hemmed in by two nearby towns and cut in half by a busy road. However, our narrow sunken lane leads off from it between high hedges bordering farm fields. These soon give way to cottages and houses, the Parish Church and the village primary school. Finally the lane ends at the manor house, which is again surrounded by fields, latticed by a network of ancient footpaths.

The school was built about a hundred years ago in a corner of one of these laneside fields. Behind the school is set the playing field, where in fine weather children can run and play, unconscious of the blessings of neighbouring fields full of ruminating cattle, waving barley or fragrant bean blossom. Set back behind the playing field, and a mirror image of it, is our tiny piece of land. Hence the necessity for a Right of Way through the farmer's field, and for a second gate to the lane, enabling us to reach it after the 200 yards walk from our home.

Fate having decreed the close proximity of schoolchildren, we felt it only natural to offer the village school (which had given both our sons an excellent start to their education) free access to our land at any time their teachers felt suitable. This they were happy to accept, though I believe they were equally pleased with the thought that their tally of lost balls would diminish significantly with us on hand to throw them back.

Returning to long-term planning, one of our earliest contacts was with the Environment Department of our local District Council. We sent off a sketch map together with written details of our conservation plans, which prompted the arrival, one rainswept August afternoon, of a young, keen and waterlogged Assistant Ecologist, Luke Williams. He splashed round the field beside me, demisting his glasses with a large handkerchief as we went along. It was great to meet someone who was prepared to visualize trees, hedges, flowers, birds and animals materializing out of the damp and empty field.

Later, while we were drying out in front of the fire at home, Luke outlined the Council Grant Aid which might be available, and would be most welcome: basically fifty per cent of the cost of trees and hedges. It was the educational potential which appealed to him most, for he had obviously also visualized future—as yet miniature—ecologists flourishing in our little patch, along with the other flora and fauna. Indeed, we ourselves had similar hopes. What point is there in preserving something for the future, if future generations have no experience of it? It is one thing for them to comment in years to come, "No doubt old meadows were rather attractive," and quite another to say, "I remember wading waist-deep in wild flowers."

This book, therefore, is intended to encourage other people to enjoy creating their own wildlife meadows. Some meadows will be larger, some smaller, but taken together they will make a difference both to our own environment and to that of the multitude of interconnecting ecological systems, which depend on these particular conditions for their very existence. It is well-known that a mature oak tree can support over 260 different kinds of insects and the many other creatures that prey on them, but I found it revealing to learn that as many as two dozen different species of insects rely on the modest oxeye daisy.

Buttercups, daisies, poppies and cornflowers can be grown in windowsill flowerpots—if that is all you have available. By half-closing your eyes and gazing at your potted countryside, it is possible to imagine that you are lying in a sunlit meadow or on a breezy hilltop. Indeed, practising on a small scale is a very useful preparation in case a plot of land should come your way in the future. Any tiny garden can have a peaceful meadow corner: it may take a year or two to establish, but then one wouldn't expect a new rose garden to be covered in blossom during its first season.

If, on the other hand, you are in the fortunate position of having a sizeable chunk of land at your disposal, and do not wish to spend every weekend shaving the lawn, nor to see it grow into an unmanageable confusion—then a meadow could be the answer for you too. Whatever your circumstances, nature will seize the opportunity to go into partnership with you, whether it be butterflies floating through an open window to pollinate your potted flowers, hedgehogs emerging from your wild corner to snuffle up slugs, or rare pine martens climbing up to dine from your bird table—should you be lucky enough to live near a forest.

However it is arguably even more important to create meadows in towns and cities than in the countryside, and by no means impossible. 'Landlife', whose address is to be found at the end of this book, specialises in such projects. The local human population has a great deal to gain from such a venture, and nature in all its forms will welcome it avidly. Green wildlife corridors already exist in built-up areas, as the view from the top of double-decker buses and high-rise blocks will show. Odd rows of overgrown back gardens, perhaps along a railway embankment, connect up with derelict building sites and school playing fields, enabling nature to maintain a tenuous hold. In some cases, like that of the flourishing urban fox, nature seems to be doing very well living cheek-by-jowl with humans. If an opportunity arises to give nature a helping hand, maybe with a small meadow, why not investigate it? After all, many wild flowers benefit from poor soil, so that rubble-strewn site might provide just the right environment for them. All told, you are likely to find that dandelions can be delightful, grasshoppers graceful, chaffinches charming and moles mysterious. There's a whole new world to be discovered, and you don't have to leave home to do it.

Ideally every street could have its own meadow: a small patch of flower-spangled grass in someone's backyard where meadow butterflies commute from the next road's green patch to pollinate cowslips, voles peer short-sightedly from their snug burrows, and children discover the miniature world unfolding before them. It is within our grasp to recapture this aspect of natural life and beauty using nothing more complicated than seeds, soil, water and patience. Such tiny grassy meadows could be strimmed flat in July, the hay saved for pet rabbits or placed on the compost heap, leaving a lawn ready for normal hard family wear, until you are ready to grow a new crop of meadow flowers and grasses the following spring.

Far from saying "this is how it should be done", this book is just an example of one way of tackling the subject. Being neither farmers nor professional gardeners we had no special equipment or expertise, and hence made plenty of mistakes. However, nothing worth having ever comes easily, and it has been well worth the effort.

We have not had long to begin to recreate a miniature slice of the landscape. Other people have done it better, and over a longer period. However we hope that by sharing our experiences of the trials and tribulations of these early years, others will be inspired to have a go themselves—rather than looking at some magnificent panorama and thinking to themselves, "We could never match that."

With the initial purchase behind us, and the subsequent planting of trees and hedging yet to come, we revelled in a honeymoon period with our little field, when there was nothing that could usefully be done, except enjoy it. This we proceeded to do with enthusiasm. The sun reappeared and everything steamed dry. We too relaxed, stretched out on the grass and let everyday concerns evaporate like the milky mists of September mornings.

Chapter 2

Soil

ALTHOUGH THIS IS THE STORY of one particular small meadow, the general principles can be applied anywhere. Part of the charm of meadows is the variety of forms in which they appear: the luxuriant flora of a water meadow, for instance, contrast with the mosaic of minuscule flowers to be found on a clifftop. There is a great variety of soil types—from wet to dry, from acid to alkaline, and with varying proportions of clay, loam and sand—which correspond to the underlying geology of the area. Neutral soil exhibits a different range of flowers to both acidic or calcareous (chalk/limestone) regions, for example. Altitude has a bearing on temperature and rainfall, which in turn produce conditions unique to each particular site.

Thus the variety of possible meadow plants is enormous. Several excellent identification textbooks—to each of which I am very grateful—are set out in the bibliography at the end of this book. For ease of reference, meadow flowers, grasses, trees and butterflies are also listed in the appendix.

Taking the wider view, meadows are under threat of 'improvement' worldwide, whether from drainage schemes, motorway expansion and building development, or the less immediately obvious but nonetheless damaging applications of pesticides and artificial fertilizers. Creating a modern environment for human beings need not necessarily result in the annihilation of other species with which we share this planet. A more balanced approach would enable increased food production, whilst still leaving areas of less intense cultivation to thrive. We would reap the immediate benefit in the refreshment of the spirit that natural beauty and wilderness brings, and tantalizingly unknown future benefits from as yet undiscovered drugs and other assets inherent in the natural world.

Limestone / Chalk

The soft white alkaline bedrocks of limestone and chalk are generally of low fertility, and therefore correspondingly high in flowering plant species as compared to the normally more dominant grasses and trees. The lack of nutrients in the soil miniaturizes the growth of these flowers and finer grasses such that, unless you wish to, there is no need to take a hay crop in July, since grazing sheep or cattle from September to March will keep the grass down sufficiently for flowers to flourish. Areas of downland are excellent examples of this habitat, rich in a multitude of flora including cowslips, bellflowers, scabious, harebells and fragrant herbs—not forgetting wild orchids.

Sandy Soil

This type of soil is porous and prone to drought; coastal sand-dunes are one example. Nevertheless even these can be reclaimed when soil-binding plants such as marram grass are allowed to establish themselves. It may well be that a meadow growing on very sandy soil requires no annual mowing, since the very low fertility restricts grasses and favours a variety of wild flowers. However, to prevent scrub formation, a cutting regime of perhaps every five to ten years might be suitable. Local conservation organisations will have the specialist knowledge for sites in your particular locality. In the event of moderately sandy soil, however, many interesting plants will thrive, including musk mallow, ladies bedstraw, bird's-foot trefoil, yarrow and the multi-coloured viper's bugloss. The appropriate drought-resistant grass/flower seed mix needs to be sown in the autumn, to take advantage of winter rainfall.

Clay

Conventional gardens on clay ground can be back-breaking to regularly dig over when wet—as sodden heavy clods cling to the spade, and bake to a hard crust during hot weather. In meadow gardens, the initial cultivation is best done in the autumn, to allow the frosts of winter to break down the clods of clay. Come spring, the soil can be crumbled by raking or harrowing to produce a fine tilth for sowing the seeds. Alternatively, you can use a no-dig system by mulching with carpet, paper, cardboard, black plastic or even corrugated iron. Although unsightly, this will save the back-breaking work by clearing off grasses; this area can then easily be planted or dug for sowing.

Any early problems will soon be forgotten, however, when the entire area is clothed in soft shades of green, gold, pink and white. Stalwarts of such meadows include pepper saxifrage, oxeye daisies, buttercups, cat's-ear and sorrel.

Loam

Loam is a rich fertile soil, the kind gardeners and farmers alike dream of possessing. Such good quality low-lying land is unlikely to be available for a wild flower meadow, and in such good soil grasses would flourish here to such an extent that flowers would become swamped. In a conventional garden, one would dig over and pull out any grass, but if you are aiming for a mixed flower/grass effect this is impractical. If you prefer to grow wild flowers without grass in a loamy herbaceous border, then of course this would be fine. Also, an area of loam soil could be set aside to act as a seed bed. If a meadow is your aim, however, the fertility can be reduced by either growing (and taking away) a crop of potatoes for a couple of seasons, by consistently removing grass cuttings or hay, or by physically removing the topsoil for use elsewhere. After these initial procedures, a splendid meadow sparkling with cowslip, campion, oxeye daisy, meadow buttercup and lady's bedstraw, followed later by the blue of field scabious and purple knapweed should result.

Acidic Meadows

Heaths and peat-bogs are examples of strongly acidic soil, but meadows with soil which is acidic to a lesser degree will support an interesting variety of wild flowers amongst their grasses, including tormentil, thyme, heath bedstraw and dainty blue harebells. The adaptable bird's-foot trefoil, yarrow and meadow buttercup are likely to prevail, with perhaps a clump of heath spotted orchid to add a touch of the exotic.

Damp Meadows

Plants in damp meadows grow tall and lush as the year progresses. This is an ideal habitat for flowers that were once common but now (with the advent of agricultural drainage schemes) becoming scarce. Fringed rosy petals of the aptly named ragged robin flowers mix with white frothy meadowsweet blooms, the pointed spears of yellow iris, and the rich gold of marsh marigolds—also known more picturesquely as kingcups.

The general characteristics of your meadow soil may well be apparent when you dig up a handful of earth: whether it is dark and crumbly, light and stony, or distinctly soggy. However, to delve a little more deeply into its composition and gain further insight into which types of flowers could be expected to do well there, a simple soil testing kit is readily available from most gardening shops.

❧ Chapter 3 ❧

Trees

BACK IN OUR LITTLE MEADOW in autumn 1991, Michael armed himself with a lethal-looking curved blade fixed to a substantial wooden handle—namely a 'slasher'. For along the field's southern edge flourished a stand of brambles and thistles some twenty yards long. There was a better clump of (tastier) blackberries at the far end, but this straggling, thistly cluster had to go in order to make room for our beech hedge. I stood well back as he wielded this blade with mediæval valour. Thorny stems fought back wildly and thistledown filled the air, but he eventually won through. There is an old saying about thistles:

> Cut in June, cut too soon;
> Cut in July, 'tis sure to die.

An interesting discovery was that these brambles had been the only thing holding up the southern barbed wire fence; it promptly fell down. This left an antique chestnut paling fence between us and the school grounds, which we judged quite sufficient. So we rolled up the ancient barbed wire and stamped it flat, for disposal at the local tip. Like the brambles, this barbed wire didn't give up without a fight, springing into ungainly and unmanageable shapes as soon as we turned our backs. In time, a wooden gate was inserted midway along this fence to connect the school grounds to our meadow, making schoolchildren's visits much easier.

In October we hired a five-horsepower digger to rotovate three sides for hedge planting in the following month, plus two rows for young trees to form a windbreak to the west, and a crescent for more trees near the eastern side. At first, the machine could barely scrape the grass off the surface, the clay beneath having been baked solid by recent sun, but after ploughing doggedly back and forth the earth became progressively easier to work. Long grass kept winding round the tines, though, as we had not thought to hire a strimmer to trim the edges first. It took two tiring Saturdays to plough the furrows we needed, but the result looked good, especially with twigs stuck in to mark where our new trees would go. "Are you replanting the rainforest?" a neighbour called over the fence. "Small is beautiful," I replied with a smile. With hindsight, it is always best to mow or mulch before rotovating—and to get the biggest rotovator you can for this kind of job (and make sure it has a reverse gear!). The job will then be much simpler.

The choice of trees in the local tree nursery's catalogue was as tempting as a freshly opened box of chocolates: native species of all shapes and sizes were available. Eventually we settled on fifty young tree whips, each about one yard (metre) high, to be protected by spirals of plastic known as rabbit collars, and bamboo canes (the former to help stop rabbits chewing the tree bark, the latter to help to support the tree initially and eventually to prevent the rabbit collar from strangling the tree as its trunk thickens).

We chose species that we could see growing in neighbouring woods and fields, including oak, chestnut, hornbeam and wild cherry, plus a few that we couldn't resist, like crab apple and copper beech. Most were to be planted some three yards (metres) apart along the Eastern and Western sides, with the remainder placed at irregular intervals along the planned hedgerows. Then we sat back and awaited delivery the following month.

When the trees and hedges arrived they looked surprisingly compact, bundled together as they were in strong plastic sacks to prevent their roots drying out. However, each time a fresh bag needed to be opened the contents seemed to expand, as tree after tiny tree was removed when a freshly-dug hole was ready to receive it. At last the final tree was planted. We straightened our aching backs and staggered down the lane for home and a hot bath.

Trees and Manure

Trees, like wildlife gardeners, need nourishment. Being wary of chemical fertilizers and keen to develop a 'back to nature' aura, we decided on horse manure for our trees—which has an indisputable aura of its own. We had transported dozens of sacks to form two heaps in good time before the trees were to be delivered, since manure apparently needs to be 'mature' (about six months old) in order not to burn the tree roots.

These heaps steamed fragrantly, nurturing a good crop of attractive but unfortunately inedible toadstools, and generally becoming part of the landscape. In fact they merged too well, going beyond normal shrinkage to total disappearance, which was the result of the work of badgers. Early autumn being a slack time for finding worms, their favourite food, they would scrape away at the manure heaps' edges to reveal succulent brandling worms, tiny but evidently tasty. Eventually only a central pillar of manure was left in each heap; in time this subsided totally, taking with it our planned treat for the trees. At least the badgers benefited.

If you want to keep manure for later use, and to stop the nutrients leaching away, cover it with sheeting, or add it to your compost.

The Trees' Progress

The following spring transformed our dauntingly dormant whips into real live trees with touchingly tender miniature green leaves. Not overnight though, as some species proved to be keener to emerge from hibernation than others. So it was some time before we could tell if they had survived the rigors of winter, not to mentioned their autumnal transplantation. Some notes on the trees' progress follow [see colour plates also].

Alders (*Alnus glutinosa*) are encouraging trees to plant, for they are likely to top thirty feet (10 metres) after twenty-five years' growth. Ours were certainly bursting out of their rabbit collars after only three years, as their trunks thickened, and they stretched skywards at a rate of one or two feet (30-60 cm.) a year. In early spring their catkins unfold like luxuriant paperchains, and their rounded leaves strain to burst forth from purple shot-silk cases. These were the first trees whose shade we were able to walk beneath on drowsy summer days.

Bird Cherry (*Prunus padus*) trees have a friendly demeanour. Not too tall, not too short, and even in their early years they produce sprays of white blossom which will dance in the buffeting spring breezes. Their shiny black fruit looks so tempting I did try eating it, but after one experiment I was more than content to leave this to the birds, whose tastes are evidently more wide-ranging than mine.

Copper Beech (*Fagus sylvatica*, 'Atropurpurea') trees are a joy to behold, but a bit of a pain to get started. Perhaps they're just not suited to our ground, even though they are reputed to like clay soil. I don't doubt that with easy access to water they cause others no trouble, but in their early years they were loath to set forth leaves, and only too eager to lose them. However they do appear sturdier each year now and their hard-won foliage—changing from ruby to burnished copper—is surely worth the effort of struggling to carry buckets of water for their thirsty roots.

It was the pink and white blossom, reminiscent of confetti-strewn church paths, that encouraged us to plant **Crab Apple** trees (*Malus sylvestris*). Compact in size and shape, these trees may grow to 30 feet (10 metres) tall, but are likely to spend most of their lives at around half this height. They are amenable to pruning, being predecessors of today's cultivated apple orchards. The small wizened fruits which result from their attractive blooms are fallen upon with delight by birds when bitter north-east winds blow across the land. Human beings also take advantage of this bounty by making crab apple jelly.

Elders (*Sambucus nigra*) are reputed to grow like weeds, and indeed these small, bushy trees are regarded as weeds by some people. Ambitious to make the potent variety of home-brewed elderberry wine (which can rival fine port when sufficiently mature), we planted a clump of five bushes to round off our north-west corner and awaited results. Honesty compels me to confess that they all sickened and died, so we shall not be putting local vineyards out of business just yet. However, for those who do succeed, the making (and of course consuming) of not only elderberry wine but also elderflower champagne can become an annual delight.

To the best of my knowledge I had never met **Field Maples** (*Acer campestre*) until we bought our little field, or if I had, we were never properly introduced. Now that we are on speaking terms, however, I am making up for lost time. This companionable little tree flourishes quietly in hedgerows; modestly sturdy, it only makes its presence felt in the autumn, when its leaves turn lemon-yellow with overnight frosts, and blaze forth the following morning like muted winter sunbeams. They are particularly 'twiggy' trees, as much of their energy seems to go into expanding sideways as upwards, but at least they do grow. What more could any new tree-planter ask?

Hornbeams (*Carpinus betulus*) are very sensual trees, growing in graceful curves and swoops rather than being boringly perpendicular. I find it almost impossible to resist stroking their dark satiny trunks, which has caused me to be the recipient of some strange looks on country walks. They are very satisfying to grow, as they produce fresh spring foliage up to a month before other species. When their leaves unfold, it is as if each one has been visited overnight by an insomniac origami enthusiast, each green oval being neatly pleated. Hornbeams catch me unawares each autumn, though, for they embody the old maxim of 'early to bed, early to rise' by being amongst the first leaves to wither, giving me a brief stab of anxiety about their apparently imminent demise. This is entirely premature, since these same leaves linger on their twigs for most of the winter.

To hunt beneath fallen crunched-copper leaves of an autumnal **Horse Chestnut** (*Aesculus hippocastrum*) tree for conkers is great fun. Scuffling feet reveal hidden treasures, as plump and polished as new leather boots, ready to be gathered, gimletted, and threaded— appropriately enough—onto leather bootlaces for playtime battles. Indeed the name 'conker' is said to derive from 'conqueror', as in William the Conqueror. Sticky buds are another feature of these trees: they herald spring when their fat buds stickily part to reveal more juicy green leaf than could ever seem possible. In fact the sticky buds are already noticeable before winter sets in, biding their time to impress a human population pining for the signs of a change of season. In later months, pink or white candelabras of flowers will decorate these same branches, standing proudly aloft, tempting one to shake a leafy hand in congratulation.

As we were not planning a plantation of **Oaks** (*Quercus* spp.), protected by silver birches or otherwise, but simply planting a few strategically for posterity, we wanted each one to be sited appropriately. The sturdiest we placed in the exposed, windswept south-west corner beside the gate—which we trust it will guard for many years to come. Growing perhaps 6" (15 cm.) a year so far, and thickening correspondingly in girth, we have hopes it will fulfil its destiny. The others also stand at various perimeter points, hopefully inspired by their majestic, far more senior, brethren beside them in the surrounding fields.

Silver Birches (*Betula pendula*) are renowned as 'nurse' trees, able to protect slower growing species such as oaks and encourage them upwards to seek the sun. Their protégés do indeed outstrip their early guardians, sometimes outliving them by centuries. However, during their own half-century of existence, silver birches live life to the full. If ever a tree was musical, it was surely a birch. Give it a fresh breeze and every branch will quiver and sway with joyful abandon to a tune only it can hear. Yet it communicates this happiness to any person who cares to lift their head from battling against the wind to stand and stare at this snowy-barked tree.

If asked to picture a lime tree prior to receiving our tree nursery catalogue, I would have visualised those lip-pursingly tart green fruits growing in Mediterranean orchards. However, our meadow has been a wonderful educational experience and I now conjure up images of the **Small-leafed Lime** (*Tilia cordata*), complete with branching stems and appropriately lime-coloured leaves emerging from gift-wrapped rosy buds. With age, these lime trees grow tall and imposing, so if I manage to rematerialize in a hundred years' time I shall no doubt have difficulty in recognizing our eager young whips; but what an interesting prospect to ponder.

The brown papery leaves of the **Sweet Chestnut** (*Castanea sativa*) linger until nearly Christmas; they look strong enough to wrap seasonal parcels in. Their flowers are surprisingly modest when compared to those of the horse chestnut, resembling unassuming strings of yellow beads, but they ripen into husks prickly enough to put a hedgehog to shame. Should you manage to prize them open, there is a tasty snack to be had. The pleasure of roasting home-grown chest-nuts by the fire still lies in the future for us, but these trees are cer-tainly no slowcoaches, so you never know.

I find it difficult to generalize about **Wild Cherry** (*Prunus avium*) trees. They are reputed to grow easily and well, as indeed one of ours did, yet a second specimen achieved very little in the way of growth for the first few years of its life, and our third one shrank. However, all three now appear to have reached a consensus on the correct direction in which to grow, and the largest delights us with a spring display of blossom tinged a delicate pink. This particular tree is given to theatrical gestures, for there is no sign of any blossom one day, yet the next day every bud has burst spectacularly open.

Wild Service Trees (*Sorbus torminalis*) are becoming scarce, so sympathetic farmers have been supplied locally with specimens to plant on their land to give this plant a stronger chance of widespread survival. Our neighbouring farmer kindly gave us three such trees, which appeared to feel immediately at home, sprouting healthily. In mature specimens, the bark peels off in patches, hence its alternative name of the chequers tree. They grow slowly, so we do not expect to be sitting in their shade for quite a while yet.

❧ Chapter 4 ❧

Wild Flowers

TWO OR THREE generations ago, many families depended directly on the land for their livelihood. Nowadays computers feature more conspicuously than cowslips as components of everyday life, but the instinctive appreciation of nature is often still handed down from parent to child. So it was in our family, and I can still recall lying face down in a field of cowslips and breathing in their scent, wading through bluebell woods, or seeking out the earliest pale yellow blooms of primroses to pick a tiny bunch for my mother. Such behaviour would cause a sharply disapproving intake of breath nowadays, as primroses have been sprayed, ploughed, dug up (and, it must be admitted, picked) to the verge of extinction. The loss of these wonderful wild flowers can, however, be compensated for by creating a suitable habitat for them in your garden.

During the first autumn we did nothing to our prospective meadow, apart from cutting the grass short in October with a Hayterette rotary mower. Doing nothing is, in fact, a good strategy at first. How else are you to know what would happen naturally? It would be a botanical disaster to plough up a field of potential wild orchids, for instance, only to re-sow with buttercups and daisies. Of course, a meadow left unmown will revert to scrub, as first coarse grasses, docks, thistles and brambles make a take-over bid, then small shrubs and bushes, until finally—about 200 years later— mature woodland is recreated. So leaving things entirely in nature's hands is not necessarily to be recommended.

When spring arrived, I began the twin tasks of investigating what flowers were already present in our little field, and which ones might suitably be added, sketching out a field plan using the fence posts as grid markers. Plodding methodically, head-down, back and forth across our field, I developed a headache—plus a nodding acquaintance with the leaves of sorrel, buttercup, plantain, dandelion, oxeye daisy, cat's-ear, clover and knapweed, noting on the master plan which species lay in which square. Cowslips were there too, not of their own accord, but planted in a spirit of optimism a month earlier.

The available mix of plants did not immediately set the heart afire with visions of blooms shimmering in the sunlight. It's difficult to get excited over plantains and dandelions, for instance, and orchids and fritillaries were plainly not going to put in an appearance just yet. Of course beauty is in the eye of the beholder, and I have occasionally seen fields so full of golden dandelions as to be almost literally stunning, but our flowers were sparsely scattered and would clearly need some encouragement.

Given a large enough area to plough, or one small enough to dig over, it is possible to begin a flowering hay meadow from scratch with appropriate supplies from a reputable wildflower seed merchant. This method would appear to have a lot to recommend it, as you can choose your favourite flower and grass mix suitable for local conditions, and having sown it according to instructions, sit back and wait for a colourful pageant to unfold before your eyes. During the first growing season, when the new growth tops 4-5 inches (10-12.5 cm.) it is advisable to firm the plants into the soil either with a roller or by treading evenly across the area. Once the greenery has sprung upwards again, mow to approximately 2 inches (5 cm.) in height and rake the clippings off; repeat the cutting each time the grass and plants reach that height, even though it will be frustrating to behead your budding flowers. This will ensure that the following summer will produce a fine show of well-rooted wild flowers amongst—rather than overwhelmed by—the meadow grasses. The regular July and October mowing regime can then begin, and in subsequent years the number of flowers will steadily increase. However, a meadow 'make-over' like that is rather costly, so we decided to wait and see how our grassy patch would develop.

Field Maple

Horse Chestnut

MEADOW
TREES
(1)

Bird Cherry

Alder

Hornbeam

Wild Cherry

Wild Service Tree

Elder

Oak

Copper Beech

MEADOW
TREES
(2)

Crab Apple

Silver Birch

Small-Leafed Lime

Sweet Chestnut

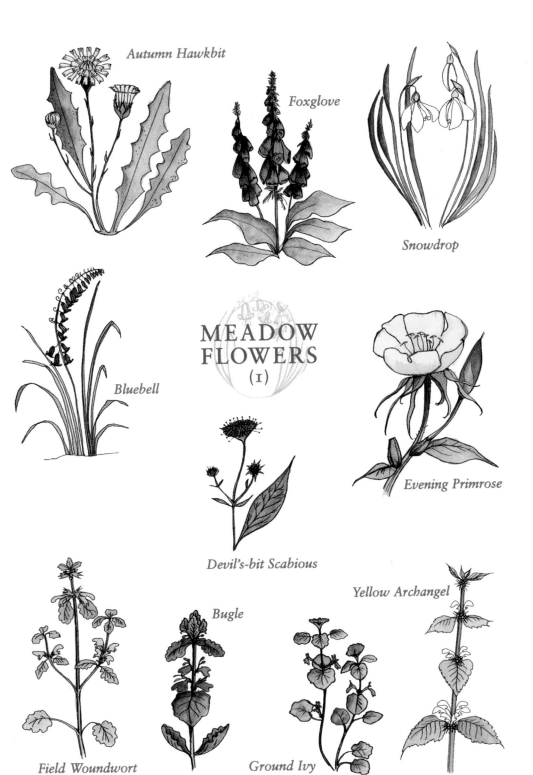

Autumn Hawkbit

Foxglove

Snowdrop

MEADOW
FLOWERS
(I)

Bluebell

Evening Primrose

Devil's-bit Scabious

Yellow Archangel

Bugle

Field Woundwort

Ground Ivy

Knapweed

Greater Stitchwort

Nettle-Leaved Bellflower

MEADOW FLOWERS
(2)

Betony

Herb-Robert

Ragged Robin

Lesser Celandine

Primrose

Red Dead-nettle

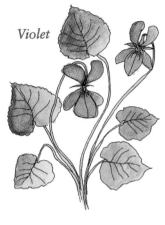

Violet

White Dead-nettle

Cow Parsley

MEADOW FLOWERS
(3)

Tormentil

Toadflax

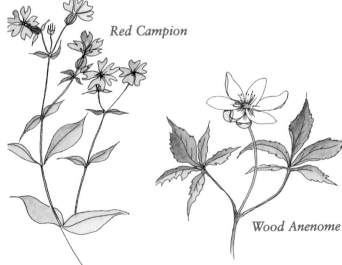

Red Campion

Wood Anenome

Painted Lady

Red Admiral

MEADOW
INSECTS
(1)

Orange Tip

Large Skipper

Small Tortoise-shell

Meadow Brown

Large White

Peacock

MEADOW
INSECTS
(2)

Ringlet

Gatekeeper

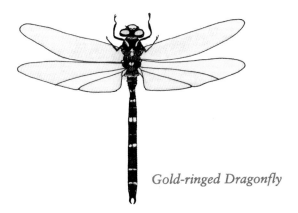

Gold-ringed Dragonfly

Large Red Damselfly

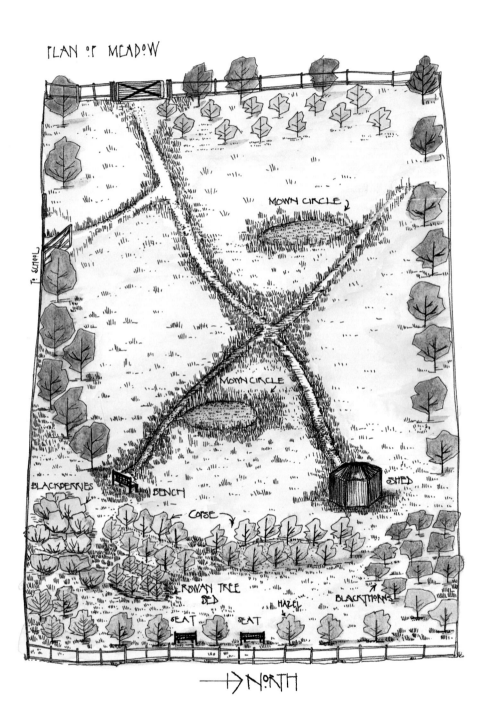

PLAN OF MEADOW

MOWN CIRCLE

MOWN CIRCLE

TO SCHOOL

BLACKBERRIES

BENCH

SHED

COPSE

ROWAN TREE
BED

HAZEL

BLACKTHORNS

SEAT

SEAT

NORTH

The first development was that it turned brown. This was somewhat alarming, and prompted an urgent study of grass types—not a subject I had given much thought to previously, grass being something that one mowed in order for children to play on. However, given its head, grass naturally develops different characteristics according to species composition, and our most predominant grass turned out to be sweet vernal, which sports brown feathery seedheads. Its name is variously attributed to a sweet taste when the stem is chewed, or a sweet smell when cut and drying as hay. Either way it sounded reassuringly rural, so we learned to love brown-tinged grass until the other greener species grew up to join it. The helpful tendency for them to appear one type at a time aided identification, until finally we had a dozen species to study. Their names were often aptly self-explanatory, including meadow foxtail, giant fescue, cocksfoot, and crested dog's-tail.

The flowers had not been idle in the mean time. Of those around the field margins I will write later, but in the field centre the first to bloom had been the locally purchased cowslip plants. A purist would call this cheating, and say that we should wait the necessary number of years for these attractive plants to reappear naturally. We knew that cowslips were native to the area, but unfortunately they are often one of the first casualties that result from changes in land management. I therefore could not resist planting some cowslip circles, and enjoyed their brave splashes of colour as their golden keys nodded in stiff spring breezes. Dandelions also appeared early, and surely would be greeted with greater appreciation were they not so prone to pop up uninvited in neat suburban flower borders. As it was, their sunburst flowerheads enlivened the all-encompassing grass considerably.

After Easter, buttercups began to bloom, both the spiky-leaved meadow buttercup and the creeping buttercup, with its more rounded leaves. By May, the grass was some 16" (40 cm.) high, and the meadow buttercups readily cleared this height in their search for the sun. The creeping buttercups lived up to their name and flowered nearer the earth, producing a softer, more muted golden glow. Later on, a few of the charmingly-named goldilocks buttercups appeared, their leaves even more rounded and with flowerheads often incomplete.

As May progressed, the attractive pink flowers of common vetch clambered their way up supportive grass stalks, to be followed later by their golden-blossomed cousins, meadow vetchling. Then the first of our oxeye daisies opened up. Soon cat's-ear flowers joined them, resembling tall and elegant dandelions, but with furry round-tipped leaves, just like the ears of a cat. Red and white clovers joined in, the red merging with the long grass, the white preferring the shorter grass of our pathways. Mouse-ear appeared too, its tiny white blooms accompanied by minute furry leaves, just the right size for a mouse's ears. Lesser trefoil, a relative of clover but with smaller leaves and tight yellow petals, crept in also, keeping unobtrusively close to the earth. Sorrel began to open wide its lofty pink spires far above other more lowly flowers. The field began to look like I had imagined it all winter.

This was, however, an illusion, for photographs taken at the time show the field to be predominantly green, albeit with gold and silver overtones. I realise this sounds obvious, as grass is the major component of a hay meadow, but the human eye singles out the flowery elements to admire and enjoy, and this is what we were seeking to emphasize. There was no shortage of grass in the surrounding farmland; indeed the entire area was sympathetically managed by local farmers. Small woods hugged local streamsides, many hedges were still intact, spraying appeared minimal and wildlife flourished, at least by twentieth century standards—although modern agriculture had taken its usual toll on the wild flower population. If we had hungry cattle to feed, no doubt the attractions of guaranteed silage production would seem inviting as compared to a risky hay crop.

When wild flowers vanish, so too do a myriad of insects and miniature ecosystems. Butterflies are the most obvious casualties, but a multitude of creatures that had time to flourish in hay meadows can no longer survive. This means that animals and birds dependent on these creatures become more scarce, and so life becomes the poorer for us all. If odd corners could become meadows again, mown in June or July and then grazed or mown in the autumn, the difference would be significant. Admittedly, ancient meadow indicator species, such as adder's-tongue fern and green-winged orchid, are unlikely to pop up, but in meadows—as in life—there surely should be room for the small and lowly as well as the rich and famous.

A field of humble buttercups and daisies in full bloom can be a splendid sight, and I have seen people stopped in their tracks, gazing in admiration at its transient beauty. It should be perfectly possible for this to be recreated. We therefore looked more closely, not only at our own meadow flowers mix, but also at those meadows owned by nature conservation trusts and the increasing number of privately-owned wildlife areas.

Dispassionate gazing showed us firstly that even the most famous areas cannot get it right all the time, and secondly that flowers occur naturally in drifts. The secret seems to be to encourage more and larger drifts of flowers, without producing an artificially concentrated appearance. Easy to say, time-consuming to produce, but enjoyable. The north-west corner of our field has the best flowery concentration, so our long-term aim is to repeat this over the entire area. Until we embarked on our meadow I had always considered myself to be a reasonably patient individual, but I must admit that having to wait for up to ten ten years to see the results of our efforts is not easy.

I will skip over the hay-cutting here (something I wish were possible in reality) as it forms part of a later chapter, and continue with our plans for meadow flowers. During the second spring some wild daffodils, planted the previous autumn, appeared. Much smaller than their domestic cousins, they nonetheless stood up to the March winds bravely, so we planted a few more. Most of the cowslips had survived the winter too, although I was not aware of this until one drizzly morning when the dandelions had closed up, leaving the previously unnoticed smaller yellow flowers still blooming: a welcome surprise on an otherwise dismal day. So we planted a few more of these also.

As spring progressed, we realized that mowing (rather than simply treading down) our meandering paths improved the appearance of our meadow. As a result of this policy I found myself preceding the mower, digging up any oxeye daisies which had been wayward enough to grow on our designated routes. These I transplanted to the field centre, together with others growing between our hedge plants, as I reasoned they would not show to full advantage there. Oxeye daisies are literally the stars of the meadows in our area. Imposing versions of the daisies that grow on almost every lawn, these 18" (45 cm.) high beauties flaunt an elegant frill of white petals around a golden pin-cushion centre. Single flowers obligingly spread out to become sturdy clumps, which sway with the summer breezes. By mid-April I had moved over three hundred daisies, so I transplanted myself to the field centre one sunny afternoon and declared it was time for a rest. This pattern of working has been repeated many times since, with bouts of frenzied activity interspersed with wonderfully lazy days, when there is nothing to do but absorb the sights, scents and sounds around us.

With summer approaching, the now familiar succession of plantain, dandelion, buttercup, vetch, daisy, cat's-ear, clover, mouse-ear, lesser trefoil and sorrel progressed. One late arrival, however, is worthy of mention. Just when all the other flowers are going over to seed, and the meadow takes on a dry, hay-like structure, there will be an overnight explosion of orange-yellow, as bird's-foot trefoil bursts into bloom. Insects love it, and the volume of their buzzing increases immediately. Any good wildlife meadow has a definite 'hum factor', where the humming of countless insects forms a sleepy, throbbing backdrop to a summer's day.

Although the transplanted daisies could be seen starring the turf in previously dull grassy patches, it became obvious that nature would need a helping hand if we wanted an improved broadleaf plant mix in the foreseeable future, so we embarked on a circle digging programme later in the summer. It was unfortunate that this coincided with a drought, causing the clay soil to resist a spade in no uncertain terms. Even when the earth was turned over in these sixty-seven hard-won 18" (45 cm.) diameter circles, the clods stubbornly refused to crumble until battered with a wood-carving mallet, to the bemusement of casual observers.

Many meadow flowers take more kindly to autumn, rather than spring, sowing. This is logical, for this is the time they would naturally have fallen to the ground and been trodden into the soil by grazing cattle. We chose oxeye daisy seeds, which if bought by the 100 gram (4 oz.) packet are very reasonably priced, and duly sprinkled these on our newly dug circles in September. Lacking cattle to tread in the seeds, or a tractor-drawn roller, I rolled them in using a kitchen rolling-pin, thereby confirming my local reputation for eccentricity.

In the third year, the wild daffodils doubled in number (which still only made about ten clumps), so in a spirit of enthusiasm I ordered a hundred more bulbs for autumn planting. Having endured wet and chilly winters, spring flowers seem doubly welcome. Nearly all of these survived, though many took a year or two more to produce flowers along with their leaves. Likewise with the cowslips: most— though not all—had again survived. With a rush of blood to the head when I saw their cheerful flowers unfurling, I blew the housekeeping money on a wheelbarrow-load more of them, making a total of about a hundred and fifty, thus producing a 'cowslip field' rather than 'a field with cowslips in it'. Such an instant result can be a real treat.

The summer meadow flowers appeared on cue. The new oxeye daisy seedlings grew apace, but were not sufficiently sturdy to flower that year. Despite this, we took heart at their healthy appearance and repeated the operation the following September, this time sowing just over a hundred square patches (a different shape, so that we could differentiate between different years' sowings). Furthermore, we widened the experiment by including seeds of some other native meadow species. It would have been pleasant to sow poppies and cornflowers but, being annuals, these need the ground to be cultivated each year in order for the seeds to germinate, something we were not able to do.

The following year, the daisy circles effervesced into bloom, their borders merging with the surrounding grasses, looking as if they'd always been there. In June, when meadow flowers are at their full height and the question of "why are we bothering with all this hard work?" seems so well-answered as to no longer require asking, it is pleasant indeed to sit in the field of an early evening. Buttercups glow, daisies seem luminous and the low-slanting rays of the setting sun turn the tall spires of sorrel into pink spun sugar—a counterpane of candy floss cast over the meadow—appearing and disappearing for a brief moment in time each day.

Meadow gardening differs from ordinary gardening in that the results bear the stamp of nature, rather than that of humans. The randomness of predation by slug, snail, bird, insect and animal, together with the vagaries of the weather, are apparent to a far greater degree than in a conventional herbaceous border and close-cut lawn. For instance, one year we were plagued with slugs crawling all over our hundred widely scattered seedling areas. The slugs were only tiny, less than one inch (2.5 cm.) in length, though judging by the amount they consumed they should have been huge. We had to sow again a month later: the seedlings only managed to grow to a quarter of an inch (0.5 cm.) before winter, and it was amazing they survived at all.

The following year I sowed into seed trays filled with peat-free compost. Although more fiddly, this method does have advantages, in that the seeds can be sown any time between spring and early autumn, and it is easier to keep the resulting seedlings watered until transplanting them when they are big enough to fend for themselves.

I list below wild flowers which feel at home in the centre of our little meadow. Only the wild daffodils and cowslips have been introduced. As you will have realized, there is nothing extraordinary here, and flowers such as these are likely to appear in any clay soil area. Specialist wild flower nurseries, whose addresses can be found at the back of this book, can supply seeds or plants (either fully grown or smaller sized 'plugs') for a variety of soil types and differing situations. So whatever your soil or position, it should be possible to choose a wonderful variety of flowers (see colour plates, and Appendices 1 & 2 for lists of species).

Bird's-foot Trefoil (*Lotus corniculatus*)
Buttercup, Creeping & Meadow (*Ranunculus repens* & *acris*)
Clover, Red & White (*Trifolium pratense* & *repens*)
Common Cat's-ear (*Hypochoeris radicata*)
Common Knapweed (*Centaurea nigra*)
Common Sorrel (*Rumex acetosa*)
Common Vetch, also known as Spring Vetch or Tare
　(*Vicia sativa*)
Cowslip (*Primula veris*)
Daffodil, Wild (*Narcissus pseudonarcissus*)
Dandelion (*Taraxacum officinale*)
Lesser Trefoil, also known as Shamrock (*Trifolium dubium*)
Meadow Vetchling (*Lathyrus pratensis*)
Mouse-ear Chickweed (*Cerastium fontanum*)
Oxeye Daisy (*Chrysanthemum leucanthemum*)
Narrow-leaved Plantain (*Plantago lanceolata*)

Buying Wildflower Seeds, Bulbs and Plants

Until recently it was very difficult to buy wildflower seeds, bulbs or plants. Now there are reliable sources where you can buy guaranteed native species (see also Appendix 5), sustainably grown and collected. Some useful addresses are given at the back of this book, and your local Wildlife Trust or conservation organisation should be able to give further advice.

Occasionally, advertisements appear for seeds or bulbs of unspecified origin. These are often cheaper, but are best avoided, since there is a good chance they have been plundered from the wild, possibly from other countries. In the latter case, any resulting flowers would in all probability be of different subspecies, and thus at odds with the aim of increasing the natural flowering ecosystems. Some garden centres may also offer dubious stock. It is better by far to seek out plants clearly labelled with their source.

Reputable firms are usually only too happy to send out catalogues, together with a list of stockists and/or mail order arrangements, on receipt of a large stamped addressed envelope. As more customers ask for wild flowers at their local garden shops or centres, demand will be stimulated and the supply will increase. At grassroots level, its quite possible that other local wildlife gardeners would be happy to exchange their spare ragged-robins, say, for your surplus kingcups.

Field Margin Flowers

Meadow flowers are the essence of summer, but hedgerow flowers brighten the days from early spring until late autumn. The following are amongst my favourites which have settled in happily with us, many along our eastern 'woodland edge' habitat. We hope they will be joined by others as time goes by. Given that we have usually been hoping to create small clumps of flowers, rather than re-seed an entire field, I have found it easiest to buy—or beg from friends' gardens about to be weeded—a few established plants and allow them to seed themselves in following years. I do sow seeds as well, some of which flourish and some of which are demolished by slugs. A philosophical and patient outlook is desirable, but a touch of desperation can creep in on some days.

Autumn Hawkbit (*Leontodon autumnalis*) belongs to the dandelion family, but is more slender and upright in its growth. Bright yellow flowers reach confidently skywards along our pathways, making me feel guilty when I behead them in the final cut of the year—although I am consoled by the knowledge that they will return next year.

Betony's (*Stachys officinalis*) furry leaves brush softly against one's legs on country walks. Their dense whorls of mauve flowers are modest in size, but they have character and the whole plant adds interest to a sunny glade.

A haze of **Bluebells** (*Hyacinthoides non-scriptus*) shimmering between sunlit tree-trunks is one of the glories of spring, with each succulent stalk carrying a complete peal of azure bells, bowing to the breeze. A nearby bluebell wood is aptly named Heaven Farm. We're still working on that particular image, but our bluebells do brighten our May mornings.

Bugle (*Ajuga reptans*) has bright blue trumpet flowers, making this plant's name easy to remember. It sends out long underground runners, so it is as well to be sure you want it in the first place. However, we welcome this cheerful extrovert.

Celandine (*Ranunculus ficaria*)—properly known as lesser celandine—either does well or refuses to appear at all; it does not believe in half-measures. The first waxy golden star is such a pleasant surprise that I bend down to admire it, only to find that an unsuspected crowd of celandine relations are clustering around the early arrival, so I step back hastily to avoid breaking up the family circle.

Cow Parsley (*Anthriscus sylvestris*) gives good value as a flowery space-filler, spreading thrusting roots and feathery leaves wherever there is bare earth for its seeds to land. Its massed white flowerheads are loved by insects, including red soldier beetles—which despite being called 'bloodsuckers' by generations of children, do not bite humans—and clouds of butterflies.

Flowers become scarcer as autumn progresses, but **Devil's-bit Scabious** (*Succisa pratensis*) fills the gap, at least as far as small copper butterflies are concerned. They haunt these blue globes with all the loyalty of members at their favourite club.

Evening Primrose (*Oenothera biennis*) bears no resemblance, nor indeed any relation, to the common primrose—except for sharing the same soft yellow petal colour. Seen at its best on warm summer evenings, the plump pointed buds, set aloft on tall stems, burst to reveal showy flowerheads designed to attract pollinating moths. By moonlight these flowers seem to glow, but by morning many will have withered and died.

It is pleasing to watch a plump bumblebee clambering inside the gaping mouth of a purple **Foxglove** (*Digitalis purpurea*) flower, hearing its buzzing become more and more muffled, before it emerges complete with pollen. Being biennials, foxgloves take two years to bloom, but their fleshy leaves and tall flowering spires are so brilliantly robust that they are well worth waiting for. It is important to bear in mind that these plants are poisonous, so toddlers should not be left near them unaccompanied. Although foxgloves grow well from seed, these plants are relatively easy to buy from garden centres, so investing in half a dozen plants two years in succession should provide you with a colourful display for the foreseeable future.

Greater Stitchwort (*Stellaria holostea*)—also known by the more evocative name of gentlemen's shirt buttons—speckles banks and hedgerows in early spring. It scrambles towards the sun on stalks thin as fuse wire.

Ground Ivy (*Glechoma hederacea*) carpeted the earth beside our blackthorn bushes right from the start, and revelled in the opportunity to spread its wings when the blackthorn was cut down. The muted purple trumpet flowers remain modestly close to the ground. Its rounded leaves, however, are rather more attention-seeking: when inadvertently trodden upon they emit a very attractive herbal aroma.

Herb-Robert (*Geranium robertianum*) may appear as a single plant in some unpromising spot one year, then the next year pop up all over. Their feathery foliage is as pleasing as their tiny pink flowers, assuming ever-deepening shades of red as summer progresses.

Knapweed (*Centaurea nigra*) is an unprepossessing name for this attractive bushy purple flower. There is a steadily advancing tide of it across our meadow each July, but after haymaking only those plants around the field margins remain. These survivors prosper, and each year bees throng around their shaving-brush petals, enthusiastically sipping nectar.

Nettle-leaved Bellflower (*Campanula trachelium*) is a member of the attractive *campanula* family. Its tall stems topped with pure blue flower-cups would be better-known were it not a shade-loving plant. So although it is often hidden from view, it makes a splendid feature and is worth seeking out.

The Romans named the **Primrose** (*Primula vulgaris*) 'prima rosa' or 'first flower'; while this might not be strictly chronologically accurate, it is certainly first on my list of favourite wild flowers. Digging up plants from the wild is illegal; although primrose plants are available in most garden shops (and this is how we obtained ours), as regards biodiversity, it is much better to collect and raise local seed— see the Bibliography for relevant reference books. I longed to see these heralds of spring among our young trees and hedges, but realised that unless I was prepared to wait until the correct degree of dappled shade was achieved beneath mature leafy branches, I would need to carefully nurture any primrose plants we might buy until such time as conditions adjusted themselves to suit. To trim encroaching long grass from around each primrose plant does not strike me as a hardship, however, but rather a price amply repaid by the pleasure of gazing at their fragrant pale golden blooms. Accordingly, I dotted primrose plants all over the meadow and now enjoy them every spring.

Ragged-Robin (*Lychnis flos-cuculi*) loves damp places, which accounts for the general demise of this once-common wild flower, as most marshy places have been drained during the past century. Its deeply divided red petals make it pretty enough to grace any garden. Ragged-Robin will prosper in meadows if it likes the feel of them, so it is well worth experimenting with a few plants in various situations.

Red Campion (*Silene dioica*) resembles Ragged-Robin, except that its petals are less deeply notched. It is also attractive enough to appear in any herbaceous border. The seeds take well and the plant is not particularly fussy about sunshine or shade, its rosy flower-heads frothing out cheerily to greet passers-by.

Red Dead-nettle (*Lamium purpureum*) is an optimistic plant, almost as likely to bloom in February or November as in summer. Although often trodden underfoot, this persevering, low-growing species is worthy of a place in a wildflower garden.

Snowdrops (*Galanthus nivalis*) are only occasionally found growing truly wild these days, but any delicate plant which can bloom in January is most welcome. The flower is well-named, its pure white central pendant tipped with green and cupped within snowy, down-curving outer petals. I have planted several clumps of these, choosing plants 'in the green' (that is with their foliage showing rather than just bare bulbs), for these stand a better chance of surviving.

Toadflax (*Linaria vulgaris*), when viewed as a single plant, is deceptively fragile in appearance, but it self-seeds so well that its clusters of miniature yellow snapdragon spires are now our familiar companions all summer long.

Tormentil (*Potentilla erecta*) is one of those resilient plants that frequently spend their lives being trodden into brick paths. However, its silvery-green leaves and soft yellow flowers also enjoy scrambling over a woodland edge habitat, given half a chance.

Violets (*Viola riviniana, V. reichenbachiana, V. odorata* and others) appear at the same time as primroses, each complementing the other by sight and scent, and indeed bravery—given the chilly weather that often accompanies their appearance. Although so small, they have the dual distinctions of a colour and a perfume being named after them. They are forever associated in my mind with a shady country lane that we like to wander down after enjoying a cream tea at a local riverside beauty spot.

The leaves of **White Dead-nettle** (*Lamium album*) do indeed resemble those of the stinging nettle (*Urtica dioica*), but as the name suggests, they do not sting. Quietly opulent hooded white flowers, set between leaf-pairs, cluster at intervals up the pink furred stem and shine out from their chosen shady habitat.

We are having difficulty establishing **Wood Anemones** (*Anemone nemorosa*) under our trees, possibly because I suspect I have inadvertently dug them up during lapses of concentration whilst looking for new places to create seed beds. However, the one specimen that was accidentally transplanted amongst the roots of a wild service tree regularly reappears each year. So I have not yet given up hope of a cluster of delicate white flowerheads nodding shyly in the breeze.

Woundwort (*Stachys sylvatica*) is likely to be growing unnoticed around the back of garden sheds and beside rubbish heaps, but when given rather more prepossessing surroundings it can be seen to full advantage. Small maroon flowerheads are held proudly aloft and add another shade to the tapestry of wild flowers growing around them.

Yellow Archangel (*Lamiastrum galeobdolon*) is a lover of shady lanes and woodland edges. Its romantically named golden trumpet flowers seem too striking to go unnoticed, although this is often their fate. Once settled in, these plants spread and flourish.

❧ Chapter 5 ❧

Hedges & Fences

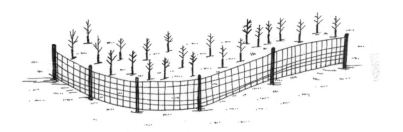

SO WHAT HAPPENED to our hedging plants, last heard of palely loitering in plastic sacks, delivered at the same time as our new trees? Most we dealt with as soon as we finished planting the trees. Working our way along a rotovated edge, we began by digging two holes. Into the first we popped a hawthorn and back-filled it with earth from the second hole as we dug it, treading the hedge plant in firmly as we went. We continued in this manner, which saves greatly on time and effort, since you only need to move each heap of earth once instead of twice, until darkness fell. Then in desperation we finished the second hedgerow by simply piercing the rotovated soil with a spade, rocking it backwards and forwards until a gap appeared in the soil, slotting in a plant and firming it down as before. It was a wonder the last plants didn't go in upside down, seeing as we were reduced to working by torchlight for the final dozen. In fact there did not appear to be any appreciable difference in subsequent growth, but I know which method I'd prefer if I was a fledgling hedge plant trying to wriggle my roots into strange soil.

Plants for the third and final hedge we left soaking overnight in numerous buckets of water in our kitchen. Entering cautiously early next morning, it was like stepping into the Everglades or some such moist and impenetrable region. I almost needed a machete to reach the teapot. However, steeling our aching backs, we set to and planted these also. We reckoned that we had dug some eight hundred holes in all for these trees and hedges, which explains why we slept very soundly that night.

Spiders were the first beneficiaries of the new hedges, working through the night to darn the twigs to the neighbouring fences with silken threads, which gleamed in the autumn sunshine. As the hedges grew, so did the variety of their inhabitants, but at first the plants just slumbered on, their thin twigs almost invisible on drizzly days. Eventually spring arrived and so did their leaves, but every plant (in their two staggered rows, each about 9" (23 cm.) from its neighbours) grew in studied isolation. There was no matey intertwining of twigs: we had to wait another couple of years for that, for these little plants had their work cut out just to survive. I don't know what they'd been led to expect in their previous nursery existence, but life on our north-facing hillside was hard. For clay is an unforgiving soil, baked hard in summer and sodden in winter.

Using herbicides seemed to be against the spirit of a nature reserve, and a combined hedge length of 140 yards is rather long to easily hand-weed, so when the grass began to grow around the hedgerow base, we left it alone. Not for long, mind you, since the hedge became engulfed by mid-summer and only a practised eye would have known it was there at all. I freely admit that we should have had a solution in mind before this became a problem, but at the time we were not fully aware of what our options might be, so we delved further into the intricacies of hedge-growing.

When planting hedges, as indeed with trees, there is the question of keeping down weeds around the new plants until their roots have become established. The most often quoted method, which is undoubtedly effective, is to spray herbicide—possibly annually— around the base of each tree or hedge. Whilst this makes commercial sense for a forester or park keeper, it is not compulsory; many people do not use herbicides or other agro-chemicals for reasons of ethics, health, or both. Creators of wildlife areas may prefer to consider the alternatives, which might require greater patience before the tree or hedge reaches maturity, but which do no harm to the environment.

Rolls of semi-permeable plastic sheeting, approximately 18" (45 cm.) wide, can be bought at garden centres or tree nurseries these days, to be laid down at planting time in order to suppress any weeds before they have a chance to grow. Starting with clear ground after the preliminary digging, this method is often effective. It is reassuring to know that rain can filter through the material, instead of having to rely on sideways osmosis, as with older impermeable plastic sheeting. However it must be added that, after a couple of years, grasses will usually have found a way to sprout through the slits left from planting.

Bark chippings are a popular mulch these days. An excellent way of reusing otherwise wasted wood, they present a pleasantly neat and natural appearance. In a year or two's time, however, even if these chippings were preceded with a herbicidal spray, grass and the tougher wild plants will have found their way through. These bark chippings incorporate themselves into the soil with seemingly amazing speed, but there is great consolation in the fact that they are improving its fertility and woodland character. Alternatively, you can spread bark chippings over the semi-permeable membrane mentioned above, to gain the benefits of both systems.

Grass or hay mulch is another possibility. With a hay meadow, this seems the logical answer. As with bark chippings, a sackful covers approximately one and a half square yards, so it all depends on whether the appropriate amount of grass or hay is available at the time. It is advisable to use rabbit collars (or plastic Tuley tubes) to keep the damp grass from young tree stems. Hay is probably less of a problem from this point of view, but on the other hand it does contain a large quantity of seeds, which could sprout up the following year.

In practice we have favoured the latter method, finding that the hay suppresses weed growth pretty well, whilst allowing sturdy wildflowers such as primroses and foxgloves to grow through. However our mulch has usually rotted down and disappeared before the new crop is ready to replace it, so some grass grows along the hedgerow anyway. It is easy, though, to keep the mulch topped up around individual trees with grass clippings from a lawn.

It is encouraging to reflect, however, that most hedges will keep on growing, be it two inches (5 cm.) a year or two feet (60 cm.). A short length of hedge can be hand-weeded, but be careful of the hedge roots; longer stretches are sometimes best left to their own devices.

After three or four years the hedge plants intertwine and shade out a good proportion of grasses growing at their base, whilst still leaving life-saving cover for small creatures.

As with all living things, a little tender loving care is required now and then. Watering is a prime example of this; unfortunately rain was in extremely short supply, since during our first two summers there was a local drought. Our little field had no water supply, and not even in my most optimistic moments could I envisage carrying sufficient buckets of water up the lane to provide our leafy hedges with what they so clearly craved. We hoped for the best and learned to study weather forecasts from a new perspective. No longer would we applaud the prospect of further sun-filled days; instead, approaching depressions would be tracked with interest and cheered on if they showed the slightest sign of heading in our direction. Eventually, of course, the weather did break, and in fact two years later the area suffered flooding. Our sloping field was not actually submerged, but every footstep produced squeaks and bubbles from fallen rain with nowhere to go.

Our 'rural hedge mix' consisted of fifty per cent hawthorn, with an assortment of dogwood, field maple, spindle and viburnum, plus a generous scattering of dog rose plants. Amongst all these the dogwood fared worst, its leaves curling up and dying at the first sign of prolonged heat. The field maple did nothing the first year, so we cut back the dead twigs and it sprouted new shoots merrily the following spring; thus proving the wisdom of advice that is often given but hard to accept: when all you want is for a hedge to grow, you should defy logic and cut it shorter. Spindle and viburnum settled in comfortably, with fresh green spindle leaves boldly putting in an early appearance from square sectioned branches, and viburnum saving its most impressive display until the autumn, when its leaves turn fiery red.

Our hawthorn was the star performer, though, providing what we needed in a rural hedge, namely twiggy thorny branches, hopefully destined to make an impenetrable boundary in years to come. However, dog rose also deserves a special mention and would in some circumstances make an excellent hedge by itself. Sturdy of growth and responsive to pruning, it does not take long before these plants are covered in a mass of beautiful pink blossom—and you are having to make a detour to avoid being speared by their thorny branches.

We had planted a beech hedge in preference to hawthorn along the southern aspect of our field, to avoid miscellaneous prickles and berries intruding through the school playing-field fence. We realized that beech would be relatively slow-growing, but were encouraged by massive beech hedges bordering the gardens of neighbouring houses. Admittedly these particular hedges had the advantage of a thirty year head start, but when you've just planted oak trees for possible future great-grandchildren to enjoy, thirty years waiting doesn't appear unreasonable.

The hawthorn hedge began to put forth new leaves in early April, but the beech hedge waited till the end of the month before unfurling—on warm sunny days we could almost watch this taking place before our eyes. For several days each pointed and polished brown bud would become more and more swollen, until bursting point was reached. Then a naked white shoot would emerge, snaking its way free, with several sets of embryo leaves alternating along its length. As these new shoots strengthened, so their fresh green leaves ventured forth to flutter in the gentle breeze. During their first few days they display a special transitory beauty, as the sun's rays shine through them with luminous intensity. Where a young copper beech tree is planted along the hedgerow its leaves also shine, but with a ruby glow—a rich centrepiece to the emerald tints beneath. The apparent delicacy of beech is deceptive, since these same leaves turn crisply bronze each autumn and hang on through wind, hail and snow until the following spring, when the whole process begins again.

There are almost as many opinions about the different ways to prune a hedge as there are different hedge plants. We proceeded with caution, snipping some three inches (7.5 cm.) off the tops initially, then pruning all twigs over about four inches (10 cm.) long in subsequent years. As the thickening and intertwining process begins to take place, we have progressed to an annual trim with shears. It is our intention to grow our hedges only as high as their accompanying fences, namely five feet (1.5 metres) tall. The prospect of climbing shaky step-ladders, shears in hand, as we grow progressively more shaky ourselves in future years, does not appeal.

Another challenge arises when we are strimming grass paths beside our hedges. Experience has shown that it is less traumatic to work with the hedge on our right, if right-handed (vice-versa if left-handed), so that the natural swing of the cutting head does not veer alarmingly towards the hedge itself.

With all this to deal with, one could perhaps be forgiven for wondering whether hedges are worth the initial effort. However, given sufficient space, hedges produce a time capsule effect around a flowering meadow, shutting out everyday hustle and bustle and instilling a sense of calm. Hedges are a lifeline for all kinds of wildlife, providing a wide range of food, foliage and habitat. As corridors for wild creatures they give safe access from one area to another. Bird nesting densities are proportionately greater in hedges than in woodlands, and they give shelter and warmth to whatever is growing within their boundaries. All told, hedges are worth their weight in gold.

Fences

Newly-planted hedges often require the protection of sturdy fencing. Our northern and eastern boundary fences are barbed wire, the original posts of which, although in better condition than their erstwhile southern companion, we found to be in various stages of decay. This gave us no immediate cause for concern, since the adjoining fields are mainly used for arable farming. However, one autumn when both our sons (Rory and Cormac) were returning home, we took advantage of their extra muscle power to replace the weakest fence posts.

We consulted the farmer first, who not only gave us his permission, but lent us the tools to do the job. He advised us to take out the old posts and insert new ones in exactly the same position, using a heavy metal stave some four feet (120 cm.) high to open up the hole. This method worked extremely well, for an extracted post leaves a cavity behind it, rather than a snapped off wooden block, as I had previously imagined. There are distinct similarities between fencing and dentistry.

We rammed home the preservative-treated posts, appropriately enough, with a heavy post-rammer, a contraption resembling a giant tin can with two vertical handles (a sledgehammer could be used instead, but it is more liable to split the wooden pole). However, on occasions when we have been inserting an odd post or two, perhaps as tree stakes, we have used a home-made wooden mallet, as described in the 'Meadow Crafts' chapter.

❧ Chapter 6 ❧

Meadow Furniture

A WALK THAT MIKE AND I PARTICULARLY ENJOY begins behind the imposing church of a nearby village and travels along a green lane, reputed to have once been a Roman road. Spring is our favourite time of year for this jaunt, as the mud underfoot is drying out, the air is washday fresh and the primroses are blossoming. So are a mass of other wild flowers, with the composition of this colourful mosaic changing according to the density of tree cover overhead and the proximity of water. Only a few houses border this track; some, of great antiquity, are gently crumbling back to the earth from which their materials originally sprung. Enveloping yew trees caress moss-covered clay tiles, oak beams silvered with age jut out at ever more acute angles, and plaster cracks widen after each successive winter, revealing fragile wattle skeletons.

Humans may have almost forgotten this lane, but not so nature. Fox and badger tracks are evident through the undergrowth, smaller creatures rustle beneath fallen leaves and birds tap, whistle and sing their way through the tree boughs in nature's version of an 'Old Time Music Hall' chorus. As the walk nears its end, high grassy banks on either side overflow with huge cushions of primroses, some with as many as a hundred blooms open at once. This bounty showers down around passers-by like a heavenly blessing, which it may indeed be, since a tiny downland church is poised at the lane end.

Further on are set a few cottages and a pub, the garden of which sports sturdy yet comfortable benches and tables. One day we were trying these out for size, together with ploughmen's lunches, when we noticed that the cottage opposite was the source of this hand-made furniture. Refreshed after our meal, we popped across to order a three-seater bench made from chestnut coppiced on the farm. There were several occasions on the walk back (which always seems longer than the walk there) when we wished we had the bench with us, to sit down upon. However, in due course it was delivered, and once set in the far corner of our little field it looked very much at home. Incidentally, a three-seater bench is long enough to lie down and go to sleep on, a handy attribute for sunny afternoons.

Seats and benches certainly make lingering in a meadow an even more pleasant experience. Depending on the situation of your meadow you may feel the necessity to embed a bench's legs in con-crete, or fix them to sunken iron bars, to prevent their unauthorised removal. Another sad comment on our times is that is advisable to chain a field gate on both the latched and hinged ends, rendering it less easy to lift off and steal.

Few people have the inclination or muscle power to shift fallen tree trunks, however, which can form useful seats, especially if you know a trained operator of a chainsaw who would be willing to trim the tree appropriately. Simple cross-sections of tree trunks, available from fire log suppliers, make excellent stools, and when they even-tually rot away too much for human comfort, they will have trans-formed themselves into a wonderful habitat for insects and mosses.

No matter how comfortable a garden bench is, there comes a time when the weather is not conducive to sitting out, and for such times a small shed to act as a hide for watching nature in all its forms is a great asset. Summer-houses, sheds, hides, greenhouses and the like, however, are less straight-forward than benches. So long as the item in question lies within the boundary of your home and garden, there should be no problem—unless it is a high-rise, multi-coloured extravaganza. In the countryside, though, even when beside other existing buildings, a new shed or similar type of construction will need planning permission.

Standard planning application forms are not normally geared to this type of request, as planning requests in relation to wildlife mead-ows are still relatively unusual. It is therefore a good idea to tele-phone your local council's Planning Department and arrange a convenient time to call and explain your proposal. Useful items to bring with you would be an Ordnance Survey map of the local area, a sketch map (drawn to scale) of the piece of land involved, an illustrated leaflet on the type of building, photographs, together with copies of any letters or documents demonstrating that yours is a genuine environmental project. Owners of neighbouring property and land are likely to be asked for their opinion by the Planning Department, as will your local Parish Council, so preparatory friendly explanations will be well worthwhile.

When our planning permission was granted, with the help of our District Councillor, we ordered a modest shed from our nearest organic farm. Not that this shed is noticeably different from any other, but the service is friendlier.

In order to raise the shed above ground level, we searched out some old railway sleepers at a local steam railway station. Here enthusiasts spend every weekend renovating the track and rolling stock until it is as resplendent as it was in its Victorian heyday. A railway sleeper is not an item to be tucked under one's arm; it took three of us to heave each of our sleepers from the car to its chosen position at the bottom corner of the field. We were in danger of succumbing to the perils of both hernia and hilarity before they were lowered into their allotted positions.

The day our shed was delivered, Mike joined our friends Paul and Bill in staggering haphazardly from the lane to the far end of our field, carrying sections of the shed between them. I hindered their progress by photographing the scene for posterity, but they bore it all with good grace as I was there to grab an end of roof or wall whenever the structure veered too wildly from the vertical. An octagonal shed (chosen for the quality of viewing it offered) will flex rather more easily than a conventional square one, having double the amount of corners to support, but we got there in the end.

We fixed inside the shed the two wooden windowboxes that came with it, to act as shelves. With the addition of chairs, a hayrake, and a battered metal chest to act both as table and storage space, we were fully furnished for all-weather observations. As they departed, our mentors advised us to secure the shed walls to metal posts sunk into the ground, as a precaution against the westerly gales which sometimes sweep across the hillside. This we did, and we also coachbolted the floor to the hefty timber beneath, and secured the roof with strong wire thrown up and over and fixed into the railway sleepers. Having taken all these precautions against the elements, we felt confident to leave our shed in the hands of providence (and prevailing winds).

Chapter 7

Haymaking

HAYMAKING IS AN IMPORTANT FEATURE of any flower meadow, and it needs careful—and early—consideration. It is pleasant to reflect that the smaller your meadow is, the smaller the size of this particular problem. If your meadow is planted in a window box—and why not, for butterflies love them—then you can shrug your shoulders and cut the hay with a pair of kitchen scissors.

Mowing half a back lawn may well only take half a day, for instance. Fortunately, the July haymaking will probably coincide conveniently with the holiday period, when short-mown grass is the order of the day—either for energetic games or for lazy sunbathing and the sipping of cool drinks. When the long grass has been cut once with either a scythe, a sturdy strimmer or a hired power-scythe, an ordinary mower will keep your now reinstated lawn neat until late autumn.

For a small meadow, hand scything—which used to be the norm—is a satisfying job if you have the right scythe, regularly sharpened. Most people, when given a scythe, hack furiously at the long grass and get hopelessly entangled and worn out. A friend of mine tells me that he once witnessed an old man cut his village green with a slow, easy rhythm, the grass falling in satisfying semicircles as he gently rotated the scythe through the still damp grass. He would stop frequently to sharpen the razor-like blade, and when finished it was as if it had been mown with a lawnmower.

The dried hay crop can be stored in large cardboard boxes in a shed to serve as a winter's supply of bedding for pet rabbits and guinea-pigs. Alternatively it can be used as a garden border mulch or, if mixed with plenty of fibrous matter, it will form a splendid compost heap. Incidentally, there are great benefits in incorporating into a garden meadow a regularly mown grass path around its perimeter and a meandering one across its centre. Not only will these be practical and aesthetically pleasing, but they will also increase habitat variation, and hence biodiversity.

A farmer is, of course, likely to have all the equipment necessary to mow a meadow, and for a medium-sized plot of land such as ours the easiest solution by far is to find a friendly farming neighbour who will be haymaking in July and could cut and bale your hay at the same time. There will, however, need to be an accessible route to your field and a gateway preferably at least twelve feet (4 metres) wide. Unfortunately access to our meadow is severely limited, and although our neighbour is both obliging and encouraging, he has changed over from hay to silage as winter fodder for his cattle, entailing different timing and equipment.

During our first year, therefore, we hired a petrol-driven strimmer. Once we got the knack of holding the machine at a suitable height, namely as close to the ground as possible, the grass fell to the earth in satisfying swathes. After raking off the hay, we went over the resulting stubble with a wheeled rotary mower. This gave a good result and would have been fine for a smaller area, but we found it tiring.

The following year we were lucky enough to be offered the loan of a flail mower. Despite its title, this machine was as docile as our friend George promised it would be. It arrived one Saturday morning in late July. George guided the machine, basically a self-propelled cylinder some four feet (120 cm.) wide, through the gateway. "How do you stop it?" was my first question. Laughing, he demonstrated, before setting off again on a trial cut across the field accompanied by Mike, whose first question had been the more positive one of "How do you start it?"

The machine made reassuringly steady, even stately, progress; in its wake lay the hay, obediently shredded into tiny pieces. With a cheery wave, George set off home. "See you in a couple of hours," he called over his shoulder. Mike was an immediate convert, cutting a neat swathe across the centre of the field and working his way steadily outwards in ever-increasing loops. This mowing pattern (as opposed to the more usual style of cutting from the field edge inwards) is advisable in order to avoid trapping and killing animals and birds (including the rare corncrake) in the final central grassy portion.

"It's great—you have a go," Mike called as he strolled past, ankle-deep in cuttings. After a brief instruction course, I too was won over by the mower with its laid-back attitude. Mike had to help me out on the corners, though, as my feet lifted clean off the ground when I leaned on the machine to try to get it to turn. However, avoiding tight angles rectified this particular complication.

For the first time we actually had fun cutting the hay, and in the process we discovered and returned ten assorted balls that had been lost by the schoolchildren. Voles and mice scattered before us all morning, but most survived. Some actually hid beside our feet, either with touching faith in our protection, or the misapprehension that we were conveniently placed trees.

When George reclaimed his mower and disappeared homeward with our thanks ringing in his ears, we surveyed the shorn field and recollected with relief that hay should lie for three days, to allow the seeds and insects to fall to the ground and for the grass to bake dry in the sun. This gave us a chance to draw breath before limbering up a new set of muscles for wielding rakes to gather up the hay.

Our friendly local tool hire centre offers two possible solutions to our haymaking dilemma. The first is an Allen power scythe, which is a wheeled mowing machine fronted by a pair of multi-toothed cutters that make short work of slicing through the tallest grass. The second is a wheeled strimmer, which cuts through grass with four swirling plastic strings. The wheels take the weight of the machine and so prevent aching arms (the bane of strimming), although the resulting cut is likely to be less smooth than that of the power scythe. We have yet to try scything our grass by hand, being loath to endanger our ankles, but I am the first to admit it is a wonderful process to watch—from a safe distance.

When I was very young we visited my great-granny in Suffolk. Looked after by Gladys, her youngest daughter, their tiny cottage overflowed with love and geraniums. One afternoon we visited the rake factory where my great-uncle worked. In an open-sided barn, a team of countrymen were busy transforming neat piles of coppiced wood poles into hay rakes. In order to obtain the traditional shape of the handle, the wood was softened in large heated vats, which smelled deliciously like raspberry jam, before being placed in jigs for bending. One end of the handle was split in two, ready to fit into the wide rake head, the wooden teeth of which were knocked into place by the oldest craftsman, who had fewer teeth in his own head than in the rake.

I'm now sorry that I didn't buy a hay rake at the time, but this would have needed an impressive amount of foresight and an equivalent quantity of pocket money, not to mention the impossibility of fitting the very long handle into our Morris 8. The modern-day wooden hay rake is neither as strong nor attractive as its rustic forebear, but even so it is reassuringly solid and comfortable to use. Raking up even half an acre of hay is very tiring on the arms. I developed 'hay-rake-elbow' but toiled steadily on, raking the hay up first into long windrows and later small haycocks.

It is easy enough to find willing customers for bales of organic hay, but unbaled hay is trickier. Initially we supplied local children with as much free bedding for their pets as they could carry. We then used as much as we could to mulch round our trees and hedges. The protective rabbit collars wound around our trees prevent the moisture-retaining mulch from harming the young tree trunks; the hedge plants don't seem to mind a six-inch (15 cm.) fluffy layer, which soon beds down.

Being high in carbon, hay is a useful ingredient in a compost heap, but on its own it takes a long time to decompose and in the process locks up vital nitrogen supplies. If you do leave a pile of hay for any length of time, when eventually moving it, bear in mind that you might disturb any creatures such as hedgehogs or slow-worms that are living inside it. The bulk of our hay crop, however, goes to a local smallholding, keeping sheep, pigs and Rosie the cow contented all winter.

Incidentally, it is well worth stocking up on sunhats at haymaking time. For with any luck you may be able to inveigle friends, neighbours and stray visitors to help out—at least until the novelty wears off for them. The force of the sun in the centre of an open field is considerable, and it would be a shame to have them keel over with sunstroke.

Autumn Mow

Depending on the weather, the grass can grow up to another six inches (15 cm.) after the July cut. If left alone, this grass would become very tangled and only coarse vegetation would manage to struggle through in the following spring. We hope our trees and hedges will soon be substantial enough to allow sheep or cattle to graze our field in the autumn—the traditional solution—but at the moment everything is still vulnerable to trampling and nibbling. A final autumn mowing is therefore a regular feature each October.

By ten in the morning on the chosen Saturday, dew was still clinging to each blade of grass, but we decided to start mowing anyway; the weather had been uncertain of late, and clouds were billowing on the horizon. This time we hired an Allen scythe, which chugged steadily forward at a relaxed pace, its twin cutters nibbling the grass neatly down to a couple of inches (5 cm.) high. There are two points to remember about this type of machine, the first being that to stop it you let go of the handle. The second point is to resist the temptation to clear cut grass off the blades while it is switched on! (The grass will fall off naturally as the machine progresses further). We took it in turns to mow to and fro, while raucous rooks and gulls followed the plough in an adjacent field which was being prepared for sowing. Whilst we took a breather, a pair of mute swans flew past, the wind whistling from their wings like the sighing of a schooner's sails. We watched silently, lost in admiration.

The following morning we began raking up the mown grass. There was no need to let it lie in order for seeds to ripen, for at this time of year most would already have done so. It would have been easier to leave the grass clippings where they fell, but this would produce a layer of fertilization all over the field, benefiting the quick-growing grass rather than the slower wild flowers, so it was hay rakes to the fore once more.

Even though the amount of grass was far smaller than in July, there was still the entire area to cover. Given the size of the field, it would have been tricky to see where we had raked and where was still to be done, had not the dewy grass changed from sparkling silver to subdued green when combed flat. Initially we raked it into rows, which were then raked up into small heaps. A tiring job, but the end result was attractive, as the field took on the appearance of an old-fashioned hay-cocked meadow.

As well as adding it to our compost heap, we spread a goodly proportion of the grass as a mulch along the hedgerows and around the trees. There it provided winter cover for small creatures and began to rot down nicely; that is, until the badgers decided to rootle it all up again in their search for worms. Still, no problem: there would be plenty more where that came from next year.

Chapter 8

Blackthorn & Hazel Copse

WHEN WE FIRST ACQUIRED OUR FIELD, the clumps of blackthorn along its eastern boundary made a welcome variation in habitat between the short grass and mature tree-line. Their plentiful production of sloes each autumn, beautiful in their own right as their opalescent blue skin catches the last rays of October sunshine, ensures the steady outward spread of the blackthorn thicket. Their thorns are particularly long and capable of inflicting painful wounds on the unwary, so their defence mechanism against both humans and large animals is impressive. However, badgers and foxes can travel their well-worn tracks where the lowest branches allow, and a multitude of smaller creatures can avail themselves of such a well-protected wildlife corridor. Blackthorn is also prolific because of its habit of sending out long, suckering underground shoots, so it is handy for sealing sizeable gaps in hedges, provided it grows in the direction you have in mind.

As time went by, it became apparent that although snowy-white blackthorn blossom is one of the first welcome intimations that spring has arrived, for the remainder of the year other types of bush would provide a more spectacular wildlife habitat. We decided, therefore, to have the blackthorn cut down and to replace it with young hazel trees, with the idea of creating a coppice. This ancient form of wood-land management, involving cutting groups of trees down to ground level on a seven-year cycle, produces a ready supply of beansticks, clothes props, hurdle staves and the like, while increasing the longevity of the trees involved. At the same time it enables woodland flora to flourish as each patch of woodland in succession is opened up to the life-giving rays of the sun, and the various stages of growth provide a variety of habitats crucial for the survival of many of our rarer species of insects.

Naturally, we were getting carried away again here, since it takes an entire wood to go into coppiced timber production, and we only had room to plant twenty-seven hazels in a curving double row. On the other hand, it was possible to see from local examples that even a single coppiced hazel tree takes only a few years to produce a fine cluster of elegant boughs.

A particularly satisfying use for such coppiced hazel wood is making a wattle fence. Providing rustic appeal has a higher priority than keeping out marauding cattle, it can be a worthwhile and enjoyable occupation to bang in sturdy posts about two yards (1.8 metres) apart, interspersed with thinner uprights about nine inches (23 cm.) apart, and weave trimmed hazel boughs in and out along the length of your required fence, one layer at a time. Aim to stagger the joins from row to row, in order to avoid weak patches. It also helps to alternate the thick and thin ends of the boughs when starting each row. Neaten the finished result with secateurs and then step back to admire your own home-grown example of appropriate technology.

Blackthorn wood is extremely tough for its size: no wonder Irish shillelaghs are fashioned from it. Having expended a fair bit of energy just cutting a small pathway into the heart of our blackthorn patch to see what it was like (even thornier than we thought), we cast around for a sympathetically inclined expert prepared to do battle on our behalf.

One sizzlingly hot day in August, we were lucky enough to be introduced to Dave, an experienced tree surgeon, who told us encouraging tales of other wildlife areas being established locally, and who didn't mind threading his way, together with his chain-saw, between our existing saplings (now three years old) and assorted patches of wild flowers.

Demolition day for the blackthorns was set for a month later, but a few days beforehand the heavens opened with a vengeance. The phone call from Dave the night prior to the due date turned out to be merely to arrange a suitable time for the following morning's visit, not to cancel it entirely, as I had feared.

Very early next day he arrived with his assistant, noted the bushes providing shelter behind our shed that we had marked with red tape for saving, then without further ado they started their chainsaw and set to work. By lunchtime they had almost finished, and we were now able to see the far edge of our meadow for the first time. It was amazing just how much space had been created.

The newly-exposed clay turned out to be very dry indeed, having been sheltered beneath those thick blackthorn bushes for so long. First we marked the intended hazel tree positions with a double curved row of bamboo canes, nipping back to survey the scene from differing angles as we worked; then began the real work of excavating twenty-seven medium holes and one large one for a rowan tree. The spade jarred painfully as we cut out these cubes of baked yellow clay. A robin followed our progress with keen attention, always hopeful of finding a quick snack.

Eventually only the largest hole (for the standard rowan we had ordered) was left to be dug, but a large, seemingly iron-hard blackthorn stump occupied the spot in question. Our stubborn refusal to acknowledge defeat led to this stump's eventual removal; the half bucket of water we poured into the hole took an hour and a half to soak through, so hard was the clay. It was well worth the effort to dig these holes early, as subsequent rain softened and crumbled the clay's arid surface within them, so they became receptive to young tree roots. All we needed now were the trees.

Hazel Coppice

Our local tree nursery is appropriately situated amongst woods, streams and pyramids of fragrant woodstakes. Arriving one damp morning in late November, we collected our twenty-seven hazel whips, one rowan tree and two dozen hedge plants. These all stowed away neatly enough except for the rowan tree which, being ten feet tall, required some intricate bending to fit into the car. With an interestingly decorated rear window and a penetrating compost-heap aroma from the damp straw packing around the tree roots, we drove home through the lanes.

The hedging plants went in first, pleasingly filling gaps along the field boundaries. Having already dug the tree holes, planting proved to be a satisfying experience. 'Spread tree roots in hole, sprinkle compost, refill hole with crumbled earth, stamp down', became a rhythmic operation as we proceeded down the eastern tree-line, with variations such as 'trip over spade' or 'collapse on compost heap' for light relief.

The hazels were about three feet (one metre) tall, with plump little green buds pondering whether to open up in the uncharacteristically mild weather. The rowan was the first 'standard' tree we had ever planted: dire warnings rang in our ears about large trees not growing nearly as well as little ones, but we felt this would be an interesting experiment, especially as we wanted it to form the focal point of a new woodland bed. Chosen because of its attractive sprays of blossom and brilliant scarlet berries, this elegant tree is excellent for wildlife (and was once also planted to deter witches).

We fixed the rowan tree to a strong stake, to keep it standing upright in gales until its roots got a proper grip. To help ourselves stand upright once more after this energetic morning, we walked across the fields to the local pub, which may explain why it subsequently took all afternoon just to put in the bamboo canes and fix the rabbit collars around the hazel trees. Although we used canes, the ideal way of supporting a young tree (if you have the resources) is to tie its trunk to a cross-bar at a point one-third the way up the tree. This allows the tree and cross-bar to move together, reducing rubbing of the trees by the ties.

Several trips up the lane with buckets of water the next day confused our neighbours, who could see the logic of watering in midsummer, but not in a damp November.

During the usual unpredictable mixture of wintry weather, our hazels and rowan tree were evidently inveigling their roots into the unpromising soil, for come the spring they all produced leaves and made themselves at home. Their home had in fact expanded since the autumn, as in March I had dug over a strip of ground five metres wide along the eastern side, joining our original crescent of trees to the new double row of hazels, but leaving a curving path down the centre, where we added two wooden seats. We hoped to be gazing across the meadow from this new spot before long.

This digging coincided with a period of torrential rain, so I became a real woman of the soil, with sticky clay half-way up my

A field mouse's view of our flower meadow

Biodiversity in action

The entrance to our meadow

A jungle of cow parsley, concealing a wildlife corridor

Newly planted tree-whips

Five-year-old trees amongst new-mown hay

An autumnal beech hedge, four years old

Bird's-foot Trefoil and Oxeye Daisy

Rosebay Willowherb

Rowan bed

A pathway through the meadow showing buttercups, daisies and sorrel

An autumnal haycocked meadow

The author taking a well-earned rest

boots and beneath my fingernails for a considerable period thereafter. This was not without its compensations, however, as after the enforced inactivity of winter it was a pleasure to be out expending energy with visible, if initially messy, results. There was the added incentive that our clumps of primroses were showing up clearly between the trees now freed of encroaching grass.

Besides planting primroses, we had scattered 'woodland mix' wildflower seeds between the hazels and around the rowan tree bed, as well as treading in foxglove seedheads last autumn. The mixed seeds grew at varying rates, red campion and garlic mustard being amongst the first to become established, with others such as violets and feverfew appearing later. The foxgloves lived up to their reputation for being swift colonizers, popping up in irregular clusters along the fence and in their hundreds in the sheltered south-east corner. Being biennials they did not flower in their first year, and by year two they had self-thinned their groups, but nonetheless bloomed magnificently.

Any freshly turned soil will throw up a crop of weeds, and ours was no exception. 'Weed' is of course a subjective term, since any wild flower—no matter how attractive—could be termed a weed by some if it turns up in the wrong place. However, I use the term here to mean a wild plant that we would not have chosen to sow. The most prominent of these, as quickly became apparent, were fat-hen and many-seeded goosefoot. These sturdy plants revelled in their new-found freedom and with their woody stems were quite a challenge to uproot. Before doing so, I tentatively nibbled their fresh green shoots and seedheads, to see how these mediæval food plants tasted. In moderation they were not unlike fresh peas, but I can't see them moving onto supermarket shelves just yet.

Far and away the winner in the colonization stakes, however, was cow parsley. From the very beginning, tiny feathery fronds sprouted through wherever there was a bare patch of earth. As the days lengthened, so did their leaves, until by May we had rechristened that eastern edge as 'the jungle'. Broad saucers of white blossom swayed in gentle unison, enticing insects to sample their nectar and thus complete pollination.

These cow parsley (or, more picturesquely, 'Queen Anne's lace') plants later took a great deal of clearing before we could plant a thousand bluebell bulbs, ordered the following autumn from a wildflower nursery. The prospect of digging a thousand holes being less than inviting, we drilled a hole through near the sharpened end of a sturdy 4' (1.2 m.) pole and inserted an 8" (20 cm.) metal bolt on which to press with a foot, thus forming a giant dibber. Even so, it proved to be a lengthy job: planting random drifts of bluebell bulbs in the chill autumn rain, whilst dreaming of hazy blue flowers in springs to come.

Clumps of snowdrops and wild daffodils were other bulbs that subsequently flourished in our new 'woodland edge' environment, their petals contrasting with the enveloping shadows and dancing in spring breezes.

Toadstools too arrive on the scene each autumn, ranging from mystically-named 'earthstars' (*Geastraceae*) to modest 'sulphur tufts' (*Hypholoma fasciculare*) and 'candle-snuff' fungi (*Xylariaceae*)—the latter's wavering spikes resembling the wicks of snuffed-out candles. The appearance of such fungi is brief, unpredictable and mysterious.

We surrounded our new hazel trees with a mulch of hay, together with grass cuttings from my parents' lawn, which we knew to be unsprayed. There's not much point in avoiding herbicides, pesticides, artificial fertilizers and the like in your own patch if you inadvertently import them from other people's garden offcuts. Recycling needs to be selective.

Another occasion when we were grateful for other people's cast-offs was when we wanted to add a mulch of fallen leaves to our copse. This improves the 'woodland edge' effect in the same way as bark chippings, but is less expensive. Our next-door neighbours were keen gatherers of leaves from their many trees, but luckily only too happy to pass on their leafy bounty to us. The leaves were particularly useful after we planted the bluebell bulbs, since even with our giant dibber it was difficult to drill a hole the required 4"- 6" (10-15 cm.) deep, as tangled tree roots lay in hiding beneath the thin topsoil, waiting to ensnare its wooden point. However, in just the one year which had elapsed between us clearing the blackthorn and planting the bluebells, the top surface of the packed clay soil had combined with fallen leaves and benefited from direct access to rain, to produce half an inch (1.25 cm.) of humus-rich topsoil. So if the bluebells were a fraction short of their required depth of soil, the application of a generous layer of fallen leaves could compensate, or so we hoped.

Chapter 9

Birds

AS THE RANGE OF HABITATS has expanded in our little field, so has the variety of bird life. The homely garden varieties we were used to living with at close quarters were more shy than normal when there was less cover initially. The tit family—**blue tit, coal tit and great tit**—kept to the tree tops until we erected a bird table complete with peanut holder, an infallible draw. Their cousins, **long-tailed tits**, we had not seen closely before, as they prefer open countryside. However, having once discovered this new source of food they were most enthusiastic customers. Travelling as ever in companionable family groups, up to five at any one time would squeeze their pink, black and white bodies complete with almost ridiculously long tails, between the squirrel-proof bars to peck delicately at their dinner, so that the peanut-holder resembled an overstuffed Victorian birdcage.

Robins have been with us from the start, ever hopeful that human activity will produce an edible snack by one means or another. If we're outside but not doing any digging, a robin will literally sing for its supper until a sandwich crust or spare sultana is produced.

Blackbirds have been able to enjoy scratching, with amazingly noisy vigour, beneath more and more leaves as time has gone by and our trees and hedges grow. **Song and mistle thrushes** too have better cover now. They use the sturdy stumps of blackthorn as anvils on which to hammer open snail shells for nutritious snacks.

Fortunately **skylarks** have always hung in the air overhead, singing their hearts out. Even though I accept that birds sing to attract a mate and to defend their territories, I cannot believe they do not also sing for joy. They certainly lift my spirits, especially on their first tentative song flights in early spring, when the sunshine is uncertain whether to break through the rain clouds and the wind still has a keen edge. Their melodious presence is proof of the turning of the seasons.

Skylark

Slipping quietly through our young hedgerows go small birds such as **hedgesparrows**—also known as **dunnocks**—and **wrens**. The bold **bullfinch** has no such modesty as he strips the tasty young buds from the blackthorn bushes each spring, the sight of his splendidly rosy waistcoat offering compensation for the vanished blossom. **Greenfinches** and **goldfinches**, on the other hand, save their finest showing until seed time. Just as the meadow is ready to be cut in July, crowds of these finches converge there, bringing their cousins the **linnets** with them for the party. Stalks of grass and meadow flowers alike bend elegantly beneath the weight of their fluttering plunderers, but there is plenty to go round. Anyone walking quietly along a path thinking of nothing in particular is likely to be startled into reality as a flock of twittering birds erupts around them.

Greenfinch

Goldfinch

Yellowhammers are just beginning to take an interest in our hedges, although it will no doubt be a while yet before their plaintive "little bit of bread and no che-ese" nesting song is heard here.

Yellowhammer

Spotted flycatchers benefit from the insects attracted to a meadow. One evening I watched a flycatcher dive again and again just above the flowers, catching insects drunk with nectar and heavy with pollen, while the meadow colours melted and merged in the sunset. The summer sky brings other pleasures too, as **swallows**, **house-martins** and finally **swifts** zip and unzip the heavens in search of manna.

Every time the neighbouring school playing field is mown, a **green woodpecker** perches on the fence to spy out newly uncovered ants' nests. The **great spotted woodpecker**, on the other hand, prefers our other fence posts, tapping in every crevice for edible morsels. We viewed

Great Spotted Woodpecker

his drilling at our bird table post with mixed feelings, as a meal for him looked like severely curtailing future meals for others, but fortunately he didn't find anything worth completely demolishing.

A smaller cousin of woodpeckers, the **nuthatch**, seeks out his food by spiralling down the trunk of an oak. Meanwhile, a **tree-creeper** spirals upwards—probing with its long curved bill beneath each protruding flake of bark. An intriguing double act.

Nuthatch

Larger birds naturally enough haunt the larger trees. **Wood-pigeons** and **stock doves** wait until the last minute before flapping away in a panic at any heavy-footed approach by humans. **Magpies, jays, jackdaws** and **carrion crows** are more proprietorial, stalking about the field like chartered surveyors, with a serious air and baggy trousers.

Magpie

Kestrels may hover overhead, especially after haymaking, seeking unwary prey—from a shiny beetle to a chubby field vole—in the newly exposed terrain. A **sparrowhawk** puts on occasional but spectacular flying displays, zooming low over our little field and performing high speed twists and turns as he seeks out small animals or birds. Yet we cannot but admire his skill and wish him good fortune as he strives to retain his place in the natural order of things, so easily overturned by human beings.

Kestrel

Migrants pay us fleeting visits: **warblers** in the spring, **fieldfares** and **redwings** in the autumn. A **nightingale** perched on the shed door once as I sat inside, scarcely daring to breathe. I hope it liked the lay of the land enough to return one day and breed.

Willow Warbler

Nature is good at surprises. One rainy, windswept evening, as I trudged across to feed the badgers, my torch illuminated a roosting **woodcock** so close to my feet I almost trod on it. I had never seen a woodcock before, so the warm brown tones of its plumage, the strikingly barred head with widely spaced eyes and poker-straight bill, etched themselves instantly into my memory. This was just as well, for after a few seconds—in which we were both equally startled—the bird shot off like an arrow into the darkness.

Woodcock

Just as differing meadows have different selections of flowers, they also display different varieties of birds. Almost any bird can turn up anywhere, given the vagaries of wind and weather, but each meadow habitat will create suitable ecological niches for particular species. For instance, **buzzards** may soar impressively above upland meadows, whilst **meadow pipits** busy themselves closer to earth. Lowland meadows are home to the **finch** family, amongst others, and are patrolled by **kestrels** and **sparrowhawks** by day and **owls** by night. Water meadows may host a clump of tall trees by the water's edge to provide a nesting site for **herons**, while **ducks** and waders patrol the area beneath. Dry, sandy meadows are the haunts of **whinchats** and perhaps even **stone curlews** with their weird yellow eyes and a call like a squeaking wheelbarrow. Grassy clifftops may well be home to **wheatears**, **gulls** and with luck the dashing **peregrine falcon**.

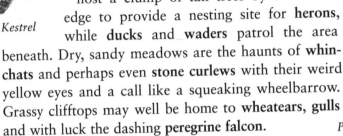

Buzzard

Kestrel

Peregrine Falcon

Nesting Birds

We have insufficient cover, as yet, for many birds to nest in our little meadow, so those that do are doubly welcome. One of the first birds to sing each spring is the **chaffinch**. Its spirited rendition challenges the sun to shine and rough winds to abate, and usually they do. It was several years, however, before we finally spotted our chaffinches' nest deep in the bramble thicket, although from the parent birds' kamikaze dives straight into the bush's thorny heart when feeding their young, we knew it must be there somewhere.

Chaffinch

A beautifully woven domed nest set in a low fork of a hornbeam tree belonged to a **wren**, who set the valley ringing as his diminutive body throbbed with song. The newly-fledged wrens resemble feathered bumblebees as they bustle along the hedgerows. Our friendly **robin's** nest site evades us still, although it must be nearby. Evidently, directness is desirable when eliciting tasty titbits, but discretion is called for when raising a family. The

Wren

Robin

neighbouring tall trees have housed various residents from year to year, ranging from marauding **magpies** and **carrion crows** to drowsily cooing **wood-pigeons**.

Blue Tit

Every spring a pair of **blue tits** have successfully raised their young in a nestbox on our shed. They usually begin gathering dried grass and thin bark peelings in early April, adding green moss and soft feathers as a lining later. Each May the day arrives when both adult birds call excitedly to one another and pop in and out of their nestbox, proud parents of their first egg. The following week the tiny round eggs speckled with brown increase in number to eight, nine or even ten, and then brooding begins in earnest. The male feeds the female and sings self-importantly from the nearby blackthorn bush.

Once the eggs hatch, however, singing time is strictly limited. The end of May and beginning of June is marked by the nestlings' squeaking cheerfully for food, until suddenly one day all is quiet. The feathered family has flown to the safety of the treetops at dawn. Our best wishes go with them.

Chapter 10

Mammals, Reptiles
& Amphibians

MEADOW-WATCHING is an international pastime. A holiday trip to a neighbouring district or country, for instance, is likely to present an opportunity to admire a fresh selection of flowering meadows. Even if it is not the flowering season, however, any meadow with a sound ecological balance will have its own particular range of resident and visiting animals to observe. This chapter describes the animals we have seen in our own small meadow, plus those you may well spot elsewhere (all measurements shown are averages).

Our seemingly bare small field has turned out to be home territory for a variety of wild creatures. For the less than energetic, it may be encouraging to note that we observed most of these whilst relaxing comfortably in quiet moments. Wildlife-watching is by no means all hard work.

Badgers (*Meles meles*; body 2'6"/75 cm., tail 7"/18 cm.) are one of Britain's most popular animals. They have broad paws and regular habits, so in suitable surroundings any track of beaten earth about four inches (10 cm.) wide and with clearance of about one foot (30 cm.) above, is likely to belong to a badger. The discovery of a badger track emerging from our blackthorn bushes was an early pleasant surprise.

Worms are their favourite food, but fruit and nuts are also popular, so we began leaving out a dish of peanuts and sultanas each evening, which was quickly cleared. I should add that the whole question of feeding badgers is controversial: some people argue that this can create dependency and encourage the animals to be less wary of humans than they normally are. However, we are of the opinion that, in moderation, supplementing their diet with foods such as sultanas and uncooked, unsalted peanuts does little harm and helps support them through the harsh months of the winter.

Naturally we were curious to see if it really was a badger eating the sultanas, since we had no wish to be nurturing a family of rats. However our customers were elusive, and it was not until our shed was installed a year later that we were able to sit and watch in comfort. Even then our evening visits were unproductive, for the actual badger sett was evidently some way off.

In April, when the weather was warmer, we determined to stay up all night if necessary to finally solve the mystery. Tucked up in sleeping bags on deckchairs, Mike and I snuggled down to wait. We were dozing off just after 10 p.m. when we were awoken by a munching sound. Fully awake now, we watched enthralled through the shed window as a fully grown badger devoured his snack with relish, overturning the dish to look for any left-overs beneath. We gave him time to trot safely away, before tiptoeing cheerily home ourselves.

Following this observation, we decided to hide the sultanas beneath the earthenware dish, rather than on top of it, so that squirrels and other animals would not get to the fruit first. Once we found the correct weight of dish this worked a treat. Subsequently, my father kindly fitted a time switch with underground wiring beneath the feeding dish, protected by a sturdy wooden block and connected to a small battery clock in the shed. When the dish is pushed off by a visiting badger, the circuit is broken and the clock stops. We have found that during the winter, badgers are likely to arrive at any time from 10.30 p.m. to 5.30 a.m., so we restrict our badger-watching to the more predictable (and warmer) summer nights, when the shorter hours of darkness bring them out between about 8.30 p.m. and midnight.

This is not to imply that badger-watching is a precise science. Many are the times we have had to give up and go home without seeing anything. However, it's well worth the effort for the occasions when we are lucky. One warm evening in July we were patiently waiting when sounds of a funfair in the nearby town made us doubt anything would appear. However at dusk a slim female badger emerged, and having nosed the dish aside, began to munch the food. Fireworks suddenly exploded in the sky above, and she ran for cover. A few minutes later she reappeared and brought a cub with her. We were glad of their prominent white face markings, as (apart from during firework displays) it was difficult to make out their furry grey bodies in the gloom. (This problem has subsequently been overcome by my father installing a subdued light, operated by a car battery, fixed inside the shed window.) The sow badger stepped back after a while, letting the youngster eat his fill, then they both trotted away across the meadow.

A large boar badger, resembling a shaggy grey doormat, then emerged from the bushes and proceeded to finish off the few sultanas that had been overlooked by the cub. His black rubbery nose detected them in no time. Then he snuffled out a few worms from the grass and strolled off into the night.

Another occasion on which Mike and I decided to go badger-watching was after the first really sunny day in May. We walked quietly up the lane at dusk, trying not to look like potential burglars. The setting sun was a purple smudge on the horizon as we settled ourselves into the shed, wrapping blankets from the tin trunk warmly around us, for the heat of the day soon dissipates. After a while our eyes adjusted to the gloom and our minds to the peace and quiet, broken only by the barking of a distant dog, and then the echoing hoot of a hunting tawny owl.

Imagination plays tricks on you at times like this. Is that something moving in the bushes, or just tall grass swaying? Is somebody lurking by the gate, or is it just the gatepost? What is that horned creature standing inside our fence? This last mirage did have some substance, for when the full moon sailed out from behind a cloud it revealed the presence of a pair of roe deer. Silhouetted against the sky, they looked magnificently mediæval and heraldic, but knowledge of the damage deer do to young trees muted our admiration. As suddenly as they had appeared, they were gone. If it had not been for hoofprints visible the following day, we could almost have put their visit down to our imagination.

The deer had arrived at 9.30 p.m.; a quarter of an hour later we were surprised to see a fox appear out of the gloom and head towards our shed. He stopped before us to nibble a few spilt titbits, but was too cautious to stay long.

Then at 10.15 p.m. a badger appeared and tipped over the earthenware dish to reveal the provisions hidden beneath. A fully-grown male, his black and white facial stripes showed up splendidly, but the rest of him can best be described as all nose and bottom, as his mobile black nose searched out every juicy morsel and his shaggy grey bottom swayed with delight as he tucked in to his supper. It took quite a while for the platter to be literally licked clean. Striding over to the birdbath, he stood up on his hind legs and lapped the water noisily, then disappeared into the bushes.

We were chilled by now, but entranced by our evening's viewing, which had made up for several other occasions when nothing turned up until after we had gone home. Indeed, we had our suspicions that animals waited until we got fed up, then rushed out to make merry in the meadow as we disappeared into the distance. Tonight, however, we went home very cheerily. Waiting for wildlife can sometimes be like waiting for a bus: nothing turns up for ages, then several arrive at once.

OTHER MAMMALS

BATS

On fine summer evenings **bats** can be seen hawking along the treeline after insects. If they fly close by it is possible to hear the soft leathery flapping of their wings. Even at such close quarters, however, I could not say what species these are, except that being small it is likely they are the commonest of bats, the **pipistrelle** (*Pipistrellus pipistrellus*). Bird-watching may have its identification problems, but bat-watching makes ornithology seem simple.

At least seventeen species of bat are recorded in Europe. Their wing-spans vary from 7½"/19 cm. to 18"/45 cm. Each individual bat consumes around a thousand mosquitoes, gnats or similar insects every night (except when hibernating in cold weather). So these creatures are beneficial to us; they are not in the least interested in tangling in human hair, or sucking our blood in a Draculean manner. They deserve to be left in peace.

RODENTS

Squirrels

Grey Squirrels (*Sciurus carolinensis*; body 10½"/27 cm., tail 8½"/22 cm.) are victims of their own success. They are to be found scampering up and down trees, whether in woodland, gardens or around a meadow. Whilst these squirrels remained shy and elusive, humans were pleased to glimpse them. Now, however, they are emboldened to such a degree that they can usually beat other wildlife to any available food supply, as well as nibbling young tree bark with sometimes lethal consequences for the tree.

Finding human beings a handy source of sustenance encouraged them to share living quarters, with an enthusiasm that was seldom shared by house-owners. Whilst admiring their cheek, we prefer our squirrels in small quantities, which in most years is what we get, and we manage to coexist amicably.

Red Squirrels (*Sciurus vulgaris*; body 9"/22 cm., tail 7"/17 cm.) enjoy greater public esteem than the greys, being less destructive and more attractive to look at—with their reddish fur and long ear tufts. If you should see a red squirrel delicately nibbling nuts from the trees around your meadow—perhaps even from your bird table or hand—then you will be lucky indeed.

Voles

Lazing on our bench one afternoon, we became aware of a small animal in the grass beneath. We had already noticed a multitude of tunnels through tangled grassy roots. Evidently this creature was one of habit, because even though it was startled by our presence, it could not quite bring itself to abandon its regular route. Again and again it returned beneath the bench: a chubby little animal with glossy fur, a short tail, a snub nose and a chirruping squeak, namely a **Field Vole** (*Microtus* *agrestis*; body 4$^{1}/_{4}$"/11 cm., tail 1$^{1}/_{2}$"/3.5 cm.). Come haymaking time, startled voles dart ahead of the mower seeking shelter. Fortunately the pace of our cutting is such that they have ample time to reach the safety of the hedgerows, although hunting kestrels and foxes no doubt thin their numbers after we have left the scene.

The **Water Vole** (*Arvicola terrestris*; body 6$^{1}/_{4}$"/16 cm., tail 3$^{1}/_{2}$"/9 cm.) is to be found throughout Britain; whilst strolling through a damp, riverside meadow, you may be fortunate enough to spot this small-eared, dark-brown furred vole taking a break from chewing bankside plants to go for a swim. This habit has earned it the misnomer of 'water-rat', but the pollution-threatened water vole has no anti-social habits and a tail approximately only half the length of its portly body (whereas a rat's tail and body are roughly the same length).

Mice

The temperate British climate suits the **Harvest Mouse** (*Micromys minutus*; body 2$^{1}/_{2}$"/6 cm., tail 2$^{3}/_{4}$"/7 cm.), though it is not present in Ireland. Its fur is russet-coloured on the back and white on the underside. This active little mouse has a long, prehensile tail, enabling it to climb corn and grass stalks both for food and to weave a wonderfully cosy domed nest. Harvest mice can be found unobtrusively dwelling in damp meadows and fields of cereal.

More slender than a vole and possessing a long tail, large eyes and ears, almost like a cartoon character, the **Wood Mouse** (*Apodemus sylvaticus*; body 3$^{1}/_{2}$"/9 cm., tail 3$^{1}/_{2}$"/9 cm.) will scurry and hop about hedgerows, gardens and fields—usually at dawn or dusk. Agile climbers, they will hang down at daring angles from birds' peanut dispensers to nibble daintily at their supper.

INSECTIVORES

Hedgehogs

Hedgehogs (*Erinaceus europaeus*; body 10"/26 cm., tail 1"/3 cm.), easily recognised by their spiny coats, are well-known for their habit of rolling themselves into a prickly ball when danger threatens; a theory which has not worked too well in practice when faced with motor vehicles. We hope hedge-hogs may become regular night-time visitors to our land, but have yet to actually spot one snuffling its way through the night. One summer's day we did find a vagrant hedgehog wandering with no visible means of support down the cen-tre of the lane. He was a determined character, declining to cross over the lane, when pointed in a sideways direction, or indeed to stay in a laneside field when picked up and deposited there. No, he was dead-set on jay-walking down the centre, and 'dead' was indeed how he was likely to end up when the first car went by. So we popped him into a bucket and took him up the lane and round into our little field, to deposit him beside the hedgehog nestbox in the centre of our log-pile. This method of transportation evidently affronted his dignity; he curled up in a ball in the long grass, and there we left him. I'm glad to say, though, that no sad flattened circle of spikes subse-quently appeared in the lane, so perhaps he is with us yet.

Shrews

Several members of the shrew family (similar to small mice) thrive in Britain and Europe, hunting insects, worms, slugs and snails.

Common Shrews (*Sorex araneus*; body 2³/4"/7 cm., tail 1¹/2"/4 cm.) are more vocal than voles, their thin high-pitched tetchy squeal-ing often emanating from clumps of long grass when they meet another shrew in their wan-derings. Small, slim creatures with pointed snouts, they live out their lives in seemingly frantic activity, but then—how do we appear to them?

The **Pygmy Shrew** (*Sorex minutus*; body 2"/5.5 cm., tail 1½"/4 cm.), a tiny member of the shrew family, is widespread in Britain. To see a family of these miniature animals floating, drowned in a garden pond, having followed their mother nose-to-tail on her travels, is one of the best incentives I know for always having shallow edges to outdoor water containers.

Moles

Widely distributed throughout most of Britain, a **Mole** (*Talpa europea*; body 5"/13 cm., tail 1¼"/3 cm.) can be welcomed into a wildlife area, whereas it might be less enthusiastically received in a conventional setting. The sight of a row of these creatures strung up on a barbed wire fence is sad indeed, but a perky specimen popping up from a heaving mound of earth for a breath of air presents a charming appearance, with its curiously naked, shovel-shaped pink front paws, black velvet coat and inquisitive nose. The fine grains of molehill earth can be put to good use in flower pots or seed beds.

LAGOMORPHS

Hares

The **Brown Hare** (*Lepus europaeus*; body 21"/55 cm., tail 3½"/9 cm.) favours quiet fields. It is easily distinguished from the smaller rabbit by its long, upright ears and energetic zig-zag leaping which leaves you feeling exhausted just watching it. It is also famed for boxing with other 'mad March hares' in spring. Young hares are born in a depression or 'form' hidden amongst grass, and are able to run shortly after birth.

Rabbits

The **Rabbit** (*Oryctolagus cuniculus*; body 16"/40 cm., tail 2^1/$_2$"/6 cm.) is a successful species, adapting well to man-made agricultural surroundings, emerging from underground communal burrows to feed on grass at dusk, and usually returning at · dawn. Its white powder-puff tail is clearly visible as it hops to safety.

RUMINANTS

Deer

Wild deer form a distinctive group of meadow visitors, with their branching antlers and elegant, long-legged bodies, as they emerge from surrounding woodland to graze.

Fallow Deer (*Dama dama*; body 6'/1.5 m., tail 8"/20 cm.) are stately animals; their impressive, flattened antlers are shed in the spring. The reddish-brown body is flecked with white spots.

Muntjac Deer (*Muntiacus reevesi*; body 3'/95 cm., tail 6"/15 cm.) are a small cinnamon-coloured breed, which were were introduced to Britain from China. with their compact antlers and curious tiny canine tusks, they are only the size of a dog—and sometimes bark.

Red Deer (*Cervus elaphus*; body 6' 6"/2 m., tail 5"/13 cm.) are an impressive sight, with their spreading antlers and powerful, russet-coloured bodies. The stags roar loudly during the mating ('rutting') season.

Roe Deer (*Capreolus capreolus*; body 4'/1.2 m., tail 1"/2.5 cm.) are found throughout mainland Britain. Roe deer are charming in appearance, with their dainty high-stepping movements, or when statuesquely posing, lost in thought, in a shaft of early morning sunlight. Some of their habits are unfortunately less charming, for in the spring they take to divesting their new antlers of the itchy velvet coating by rubbing them vigorously against young whippy branches, leaving frayed bark and thus severely pruned trees. However, as infrequent visitors content to put in occasional celebrity appearances, they make a thrilling sight as they leap gracefully over the gate to browse.

Sika Deer (*Cervus nippon*; body 4'/1.2 m., tail 6" /15 cm.) have chestnut coats sprinkled with white spots. Introduced originally from Japan, they are now widespread throughout Britain. Perhaps their most striking feature is their loud whistling during the mating season.

CARNIVORES

Canines

The **Red Fox** (*Vulpes vulpes*; body 2' 6"/75 cm., tail 18"/45 cm.) is native throughout Britain. The first fox to visit us was a young cub in early September. His auburn fur fluffed up in the sunshine as he optimistically stalked a dim-witted pheasant which had taken to relaxing behind our bench. At the last moment the pheasant exploded into the air with a flurry of feathers and shrieks of alarm, leaving the fox cub feeling both foolish and hungry. No doubt he improved with practice though, as full-grown foxes do put in an appearance from time to time. They pace purposefully about their business until suddenly aware that they are being observed.

This does not prompt an immediate dash for safety, but a haughty stare in our direction, followed by a steady trot towards cover.

Weasels

Resident in Wales (and much of mainland Europe), the **Western Polecat** (*Mustela putorius*; body 16"/40 cm., tail 6"/15 cm.) is related to the stoat and weasel, but is larger and heavier. Lavishly fur-coated, they hunt mainly at night, but are also active at dawn and dusk, hunting rodents, birds and frogs.

Stoats (*Mustela erminea*; body 10"/25 cm., tail 4¾"/12 cm.) are resident throughout Britain. A stoat will stalk, then pounce upon mice, voles and rabbits, so it is likely to be chanced upon in meadows. Bounding energetically through long grass, the black tip of its tail contrasts with its brown and white (in winter sometimes totally white) body fur.

Weasels (*Mustela nivalis*; body 8"/20 cm., tail 2"/5 cm.) are widely distributed in mainland Britain. Undulating along the ground, a weasel can resemble an overfed, furry, chestnut-coloured caterpillar with a white underbody. When hunting, it is slim enough to creep into the tunnels of small rodents, who find the weasel a terrifying foe.

REPTILES

Lizards

Lizards (*Lacerta vivipara*; body and tail 5"/13 cm.) are, like us, tempted out by the tentative rays of March sunshine—in our case, bringing the deckchairs out of the shed for an airing, even though while sitting in them we'll probably still be wearing our thick winter jackets. The grass mulch along the hedgerows has taken on a bronze hue over the winter, which almost exactly matches the lizard's smooth skin, so it is not until the animal flicks its tail that we notice its presence beside us. The three of us exchange glances before settling down to sunbathe, different creatures united in the need for warmth.

Although the **Slow-worm** (*Anguis fragilis*; body and tail 16"/40 cm.) resembles a smoothly metallic silvery or bronze snake, their zoological classification is the interestingly inebriated one of legless lizard. Widely distributed throughout Britain and Europe, slow-worms quietly inhabit gardens and secluded meadows, hiding beneath stones, logs or compost heaps—emerging to bask in the early morning sun, or to seek food (worms, slugs and snails) of an evening, particularly after a shower of rain. Like other lizards, slow-worms can escape danger when caught by shedding their tail, which subsequently re-grows, although in a shortened version.

Snakes

Olive-green or brown in colour, with a yellow and black collar and half-bars of black at intervals along its body, the **Grass Snake** (*Natrix natrix*; body and tail 4'/1.2 m.) is widespread throughout most of Britain and Europe. Grass snakes prefer to live beside lakes and ponds: they are excellent swimmers, devouring large numbers of fish and frogs. When cornered, a grass snake may hiss and even strike—usually with its mouth closed—but they are not venomous to humans.

AMPHIBIANS

Frogs

The **Common Frog** (*Rana temporaria*; body 2¾"/7 cm.) is to be found near water across Britain, Northern and Central Europe; these smooth-skinned, leaping amphibians which develop from tadpoles, are well-known to most youngsters. The fact that we decided not to include a pond in our field plan may appear surprising, since there is no doubt that water attracts a wide range of wildlife. However, water also has a fascination for children, and with an adjoining primary school this did not seem wise. Also there are several ponds in the vicinity, including a small, supervised pond in the school grounds. Perhaps as a consequence of this, we are not short of frogs in our meadow. Crouched beside the log pile, or lingering in shady nooks and crannies, frogs of varying sizes materialize suddenly and silently. Their colour also varies, from yellow to green to almost black, depending on their habitat. How long does it take a frog to adjust, chameleon-like, to its surroundings, I wonder?

Toads

Toads are generally larger, drier creatures than frogs, and liberally sprinkled with warts. Folklore describes their large protuberant eyes as hidden jewels, causing a good few unfortunate toads to have been slaughtered in the past. However **Common Toads** (*Bufo bufo*; body 4³/4"/12 cm.) live in peace with human beings these days, dwelling in cool hollows for up to forty years, devouring worms, slugs and passing insects, and croaking musically during refreshing showers of rain.

From all this, it can be seen that meadows are a hive of activity. Yet despite the greater size of these creatures, they are each dependent upon the humblest plants and smallest insects at the beginning of their food chain. Nothing can exist in isolation.

Chapter 11

Insects

BUTTERFLIES ARE SURELY amongst the most graceful of insects. Like delicate pairs of painted petals, far too beautiful to have been the product of any human hand, these miniature masterpieces of nature's design flutter joyfully through fields and gardens.

Here in our little field [see colour plates], **Small Tortoise-shell** (*Aglais urticae*) butterflies are the first to greet the spring sunshine. They deserve to be prolific, since mating is their major preoccupation. Nuptial pairs spiral skywards, lost in mutual passion. I even saw one hopeful male pursue a bumblebee, but he returned shortly afterwards, suitably chastened.

Orange Tip (*Anthocharis cardamines*) butterflies love milkmaids (cuckoo flowers), choosing these pale pinky-mauve blossoming plants to lay their eggs upon. Given a damp spot—in spring, few spots are not—and some turned earth, milkmaid plants seed themselves as if there was no tomorrow, so if all goes well these delicate butterflies are regular early visitors.

Peacock (*Inachis io*) butterflies are another early arrival on the scene. Like their namesake, they appear to welcome the limelight, displaying proudly in any sheltered sunny spot, delighting in snapping their wings shut just as anyone creeps near enough to take a photograph.

Both **Large White** (*Pieris brassicae*) and **Small White** (*Pieris rapae*) butterflies appear in May, sipping nectar from the buttercups and daisies; their **Green-veined White** (*Pieris napi*) cousins float amongst the cow parsley. Whilst the caterpillars of both the Large and Small White are to be found munching their way through cabbages, these are the only European species of butterfly to do so; most prefer innocuous nurseries for their young amongst such plants as stinging nettles, wild flowers and grasses.

June sees the arrival of **Meadow Browns** (*Maniola jurtina*). They soon become a feature of the field, fluttering companionably by as we stroll along the grassy paths. **Large Skippers** (*Ochlodes venata*)— which are, in fact, rather small—arrive next, resting only briefly between their jaunts from flower to flower, before skipping on to the next.

The pale pink blooms of the bramble patch act as a magnet to late summer butterflies. **Ringlets** (*Aphantopus hyperantus*), **Gatekeepers** (*Pyronia tithonus*) and **Red Admirals** (*Vanessa atalanta*) cluster there making the most of each moment.

So much for our regulars, but butterflies surf international air currents as enthusiastically as avid computer-users surf the Internet. So while each country has its regularly occurring species, almost any butterfly may unexpectedly arrive on favourable winds; in our meadow, another half-a-dozen species appear and disappear from time to time. One summer we were inundated with so many **Painted Ladies** (*Cynthis cardui*) that the whole field shimmered with them.

Possible butterfly visitors to British and American meadows are listed in the back of the book, together with examples of the plant families that their caterpillars prefer to feed on.

Bees, when they're not being pursued by amorous tortoise-shell butterflies, also revel in meadows, be they large or small. We have four regular types: **Buff-tailed** (*Bombus terristris*) and **Red-tailed** (*Bombus lapidarius*), whose common names are self-explanatory, **Carder Bees** (*Bombus pascorum*), which look as if they are wearing ginger woolly cardigans, and finally **Honey Bees** (*Apis mellifera*). We also play host to numerous **Hover-flies** and **Wasps.** Given a good insect identification book, an entire summer could be spent deciphering the Morse code of dots and dashes on these creatures.

Buff-tailed Bumblebee

Some beetles are spectacularly shaped and coloured, like the magnificently horned **Stag Beetle** (*Lucanus*

Stag Beetle

cervus)—occasionally to be found on ancient oak trees—and the appropriately-named **Red-robed Cardinal Beetle** (*Pyrochroa coccinea*), which has a weakness for hawthorn blossom. **Moths** are a whole secret tribe, appearing of an evening in apparently muted colours, yet sometimes displaying bright flashes of vivid designs to rival their butterfly cousins. **Dragonflies** and **Damsel-flies** flaunt themselves

Emperor Dragonfly

boldly, shimmering amongst the bushes like fragmented rainbows. The dragonflies hold their wings outstretched even when at rest, while the daintier damsel-flies fold them neatly along their backs.

One of the traditional sounds of summer is that of **Grasshoppers** (*Chorthippus brunneus*) typing industriously in the lengthening grass. Dashing off quick letters to the Environment Ministry about meadow preservation, perhaps?

Common Field Grasshopper

Hundreds of different types of birds visit Britain, and there must be thousands of species and subspecies of wild flowers, so I'm prepared to believe there could be millions of insect species. Indeed there are estimated to be a quarter of a million individual insects per acre of grassland. Yes, insects are certainly fascinating, but as yet no-one has given me a microscope to discover them all, and sometimes I think it is just as well!

Chapter 12

Schoolchildren's Visits

WHILST BEING GUIDED along the educational path, children at the village school discover that lessons can proceed in a multitude of fascinating guises, with plenty of opportunities to exercise youthful high spirits. We were happy to become part of this process.

The first class to visit us was, appropriately enough, the youngest. Their classroom topic was 'animal homes' and we were to provide the fieldwork. A group tour of inspection began with a hedgehog nestbox in our log pile. Being early October there was no hedgehog in residence, but a multitude of woodlice, beetles and worms hiding beneath the logs were greeted with great enthusiasm by the children and carried carefully to their long-suffering teachers. Oak galls on low branches were displayed as now empty homes of gall wasp grubs, and the tale of how I was hoeing the hedgerow only to disturb a bees nest and have to run for shelter caused several children to request a repeat performance. Spiders' webs were conveniently located at child height along the fence, together with a mysterious small tunnel dug beside a fencepost, for which guesses were invited as to what creature might live there.

The badgers' tunnel through the impenetrable blackthorn bushes was peered down with interest, and proof of ownership had been kindly supplied the previous night when a badger left a clear broad pawprint in a patch of sand placed near the sultanas dish for that very purpose. The successful expedition returned cheerfully to the classroom to discuss and draw their discoveries.

In early December we replanted some of our sturdiest new trees with each school class. The weather was dull, but the atmosphere was very cheerful as we inserted trees, shovelled and stamped earth, applied bamboo canes and rabbit-collars, and fell down holes. Luke Williams, the Assistant Ecologist, duly arrived to capture the moment on video. I gave every child an acorn to plant in their own gardens, but the most popular moment was when I gave out sweets as a reward for a job well done.

To give central points of interest to the two 'sitting down circles' mown in summer for the schoolchildren beside the grass paths, we thought simple sculptures would be fun. Accordingly we visited the local garden centre and studied their rockery stones. Lacking a supply of marble, or Leonardo da Vinci to go with it, we plumped for two giant pebbles, each about a foot in length. This involved lining up a variety of pebbles to study through half-closed eyes, from various angles, to see if they resembled any animal shapes. It tended to confuse passing sales assistants.

Eventually, however, we settled on our two pebbles and took them home for painting. One was destined to become a rabbit, the other a badger cub. Mike christened the badger Rocky, which inevitably led to us calling the rabbit Roxy. They were far from fine art, but jolly, and the children approved.

A class of seven-year-olds visited in June. Perched on and around the bench and table, the children enthusiastically volunteered news about nature they had observed in their own gardens, then asked all manner of questions on topics from butterflies to badgers, toadstools to trees, plus everything else in between. Then they all went off to seek things out for themselves. I was kindly invited into their classroom later to see the impressive results of their efforts, where paintings, poems and prose adorned the walls in profusion.

As a result of being able to keep fairly accurate records of when our badgers appeared for their supper, we were able to offer the schoolchildren the opportunity to come badger-watching with their mothers in the summer. This was on the understanding that they might well have to sit still for an hour and even then perhaps not see anything. Some of the first pupils to take us up on this were Danielle and Jenni and their mums.

We were expecting the badger to arrive about 10.00 p.m., going on current form, but when we arrived at 9.00 p.m. our regular visiting badger was already at the dishes. She ran off on seeing us and we tiptoed into the shed hoping for her return. An hour later we were just about to give up and go home, when not one but two badgers arrived. They put on a great show between them, munching happily, strolling around and drinking water from the bird-bath. An entertaining half-hour which we all enjoyed, not least the badgers.

Over the years, thanks to the inventiveness of their teachers, local children's lessons have benefited in many ways from our little area of wilderness. Natural history study might well have been anticipated, but scientific experiments, plus mathematical calculations such as working out the average height of a clump of lofty teasels, were more unexpected.

Projects such as inventing plans for new nature reserves, produced some very comprehensive schemes with innovative ideas from the children. We've been included in an orienteering exercise and a geography video. Map-making of half-an-acre is not as simple as it sounds when the grass is half as tall as you are and it is impossible to get a clear view from one end of the field to the other. Art and creative writing sessions have produced many a masterpiece, when opportunities have been perceptively offered by teachers for children to stop, look and listen to the natural world.

Chapter 13

Meadow Crafts

A WILDLIFE MEADOW brings with it several fringe benefits, including craft materials such as teasels or corn, which might not otherwise come readily to hand. It also provides an opportunity to experiment with free-style carpentry for the benefit of visitors, both humans and wild creatures. The following pages give some suggestions for craft work. Your own particular circumstances will probably spark off ideas for other projects such as dried flower pictures, rush mats and twig baskets, or transforming windblown timber into creative carvings.

Wooden Mallet

Occasionally you may have to cut down a sm tree, perhaps to clear an overgrown area. This proj enables the timber to be put to good use.

Saw through a tree-trunk of about 4" (10 cn diameter, some 3" (7.5 cm.) both above and below junction with a strong straight branch, approximate 4' (120 cm.) in length. The resulting mallet make very useful tool for driving in tree stakes, etc., a could even be used for croquet when the hay has be cut.

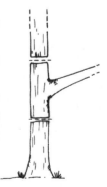

Post-Holder

This gadget is designed to aid the unfortunate person who has drawn the short straw in a post-erecting operation—and has to hold the post steady whilst a companion wields the mallet with gusto.

1. Hinge together two lengths of wood, each 3' 6" x 2½" x 1" (115 cm. x 6 cm. x 2.5 cm.).

2. Screw a 2½" x 1" x 1" (6 cm. x 2.5 cm. x 2.5 cm.) length of wood some 7" (17.5 cm.) from the hinge across the inside top of one handle.

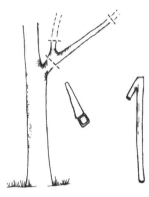

3. Screw a second 2½" (6 cm.) length of wood about 8" (20 cm.) fr[...] across the inside top of the [...] dle, so that it rests beneat[...] cross-piece.

4. Grip the post nutcracl[...] ion, between the two handles. (The two pieces will prevent the post slipping towar[...] you.)

You will now be a safer distance away when the post is knocked in.

Walking Stick

Trimmed branches can be put to good use by turning them into walking sticks. Choose a long straight branch joined by a slightly thinner one. Cut through below their joint, then cut 4" (10 cm.) above it on the thinner branch. Trim the thicker branch to the length you find most comfortable for walking with.

A walking stick with a handle like this is very useful for pulling down

bramble sprays to pick blackberries, or for hauling yourself
out of a ditch should you happen to fall in.

If you are coppicing a hazel tree, try planting a honeysuckle
beside it. As both plants grow, gently twist the honeysuckle
around a suitable hazel shoot and wait a few years. When the hazel
is an appropriate size for a walking stick, cut it down and unwind
the honeysuckle. With luck you will find that the wood has an attractive barley sugar twist all the way up.

Quadrat

When estimating plant species density, botanists are prone to toss
a wooden quadrat frame, 1 metre square, over their shoulder and
then count the types and numbers of plants found growing within its
randomly enfolding boundaries. It is probably safer to drop a
quadrat in front of you, for fear of repercussions from passers-by,
but the frame itself is relatively uncomplicated.

1. Saw four lengths of wood 3' 5" x 1" x $^{1}/_{4}$" (105 cm. x 2.5 cm. x
0.625 cm.)

2. Drill a central hole $^{1}/_{2}$" (1.25 cm.) away from
each of the eight ends.

3. Place wood into a square outline, overlap corners and join with a
1 $^{1}/_{4}$" (3 cm.) length bolt and butterfly nut.

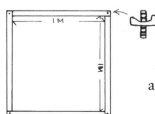

4. These nuts can be easily
adjusted to make a firm
square shape, or loosened in
order to fold the quadrat
away for storage.

Bird Nestbox

1. Saw the nestbox sections as shown in the diagram below, from 3/4" (2 cm.) thick planed softwood, except for base section. (Leave sawing this part until you finally fix the box together, as wood thickness may vary and this might create a gap at the base.)

	40 cm.	25 cm.	25 cm.	20 cm.	22.5 cm.	11 cm.	
6"	back	front	side	side	roof	base	15 cm.
	16"	8"	8"	10"	9"	4¹/₂"	

2. Drill entrance hole: 1" (2.5 cm.) in diameter for blue and coal tits, 1¹/8" (2.75 cm.) for great tits.

3. Nail (or drill and screw) the sides and front section together.

4. Drill a fixing hole top and bottom of back panel, then nail or drill and screw sides to back section.

5. Check size of nestbox floor, cut out and fix in.

6. Surform or sandpaper top edge of roof to an angle for a better fit, then tack on a 2" (5 cm.) wide strip of rubber from an old wellington boot to secure the roof to the back, producing a waterproof hinge.

7. Fix a small hook and eye to each side of the lid to prevent it being lifted by wind or squirrels.

8. Erect nestbox, preferably in the autumn, about 6' (2 metres) high and out of cats' leaping range (birds start prospecting for a nest site in January). It should face away from the hot southerly sun and westerly rain.

N.B. Do not use any preservative as this would be dangerous to the health of the birds.

Bat Box

Bats are so threatened by toxic insecticides that they need all the help they can get. A bat box can be made from untreated, preferably rough-sawn timber, along very similar lines to the bird nestbox. There is no front entrance hole, but instead a 3/4" (2 cm.) base entry slit.

	40 cm.	20 cm.	25 cm.	20 cm.	22.5 cm.	4.5 cm.	
6"	back	front	side	side	roof	b a s e	15 cm.
	16"	5"	8"	10"	9"	3³/₄"	

Before fixing the wooden sections together, panel-pin or drill and screw two bat perches against the inside of the back wall. These are made of wood ¹/₂" (1.25 cm.) square and 4" (10 cm.) long.

The hinge is once again made from a strip of rubber cut from an old wellington boot and tacked on to the roof and back panel, forming a weatherproof joint.

Two hooks and eyes should be used to secure either side of the roof against wind and squirrels. Bats are protected by law, and so although a hinged roof is useful, casual inspections should not be carried out.

Bats prefer to roost high off the ground (think of a church belfry, for instance). So a position about 6 yards (metres) high on a wall or tree trunk would be ideal. However, if this is not possible, it is worth experimenting at lower levels. When siting the bat box, avoid facing it due east or west.

Nestbox Periscope

If a nestbox is attached over a shed window, it is possible to incorporate a piece of clear perspex about 4" (10 cm.) square in the rear panel of the nestbox. Naturally, birds will not enter if light is coming into the box, but a periscope fixed to the window frame will allow occasional discreet observation. Please remember that the birds' welfare always comes first.

1. Saw the hardboard sections and lengths of 3/4" (2 cm.) square pine as shown in the diagram below.

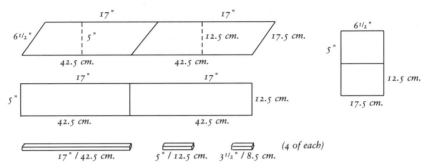

2. Fix a small mirror (stainless steel ones sold in camping shops are ideal) to each of the sloping end pieces, then panel-pin and wood glue the sections together. Seal any gaps.

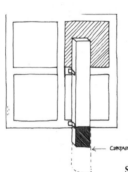

3. Fix periscope to wall or window frame by means of brackets. Seal any gaps around the top with 2" (5 cm.) wide waterproof tape.

4. Add a small thick curtain to the lower open end of the periscope and only fold this back when in use. A second, larger curtain, fitted above the first to drape over your head and shoulders during observations, will stop stray light intruding inside the nestbox.

Mouse Box

If you come across a fallen hollow branch nestling picturesquely on a mossy bank surrounded by leaves, obviously it is already an ideal home for a small mammal and should be left alone. However, if you find a hollow branch fallen onto concrete, or in your latest delivery of logs for the fire, it may be possible to nail on a rear wooden panel, and a smaller front panel, but leave an

entry space. Finally, fill the log
with hay or dry leaves.

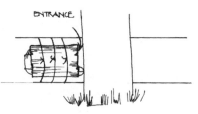

Unlike a bird nestbox,
the entrance should be
positioned facing inwards,
about 1" (2.5 cm.) from a fence
post or tree trunk. Secure the mouse box with loops of galvanised
wire. A few hazelnuts or peanuts can be popped inside as an additional encouragement to any prospective tenant.

Hedgehog Box

A wooden box about 14" x 12" (35 cm. x 30 cm.) by 6" (15 cm.)
high, constructed from 3/4" (2 cm.) thick wood, makes a safe retreat

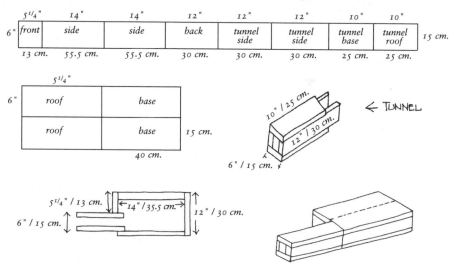

for a hedgehog to nest or hibernate in, provided it is placed in a suitably secluded position—perhaps beneath a pile of logs in a sheltered
corner. An entrance tunnel about 6" (15 cm.) square and 10" (25
cm.) long will enable the hedgehog to feel more secure from intruders.

The wood should not be treated with preservative, as hedgehogs
have an acute sense of smell; besides which, if beetles and grubs do
invade the box, the hedgehog can enjoy breakfast in bed. Fill the
completed box with hay or dried leaves.

Bird Table

A bird table is an infallible way of attracting wild birds, but care is required when deciding where to site it. Cats are the main danger, I once saw one lean across from the top of a wall to rest its head on a bird table, apparently thinking it merely had to open its mouth for the birds to walk in.

The RSPB (see Useful Addresses at the back of this book) sells bird tables and feeding devices of all descriptions, but it is both possible and pleasing to make your own. Basically you need a flat wooden tray with raised edges to stop food blowing off, but with gaps at each corner to let the rain drain away. Five-ply wood is suitable for

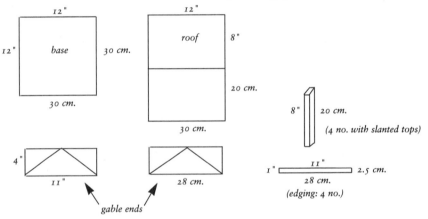

gable ends

the roof and base, provided you treat it with at least two coats of wood-preservative when the project is completed. The four triangular offcuts from the inset gable ends of the roof can be used as extra supporting struts between the table base and the post. Corner-posts are made from 1" x 1" (2.5 cm. x 2.5 cm.) timber, each approximately 8" (20 cm.) high.

You'll probably want the bird table to be convenient for easy observation. Access is important too, since you will doubtless be refilling the food stocks daily, as birds will become reliant on your generosity, particularly in severe weather, in order to survive. However, do make sure that cats cannot hide within leaping distance of the food supply.

Bird Table Accessories

A squirrel-proof (metal) peanut-dispenser can be hung from the bird table roof. If you use a fixing bracket for this, be sure it has rounded ends and is not likely to poke anyone in the eye. Pesticide-free peanuts can be obtained nowadays from the RSPB, specialist mail-order firms, some pet shops and garden centres.

Around Christmas there is likely to be a wider selection of nuts available, so you may wish to share this variety with the birds and perhaps attract a woodpecker or two. Find a log about 8" (20 cm.) long and drill holes about half-an-inch (1.25 cm.) in both width and depth at random intervals. Fill these with shelled Brazil, hazel and almond nuts and hang from the bird table roof. Come the New Year, try filling these holes with peanut-butter or suet instead and there should be a steady stream of peckish customers.

Wild bird seeds together with scraps of bread, cheese and bacon rind will all be well received by the birds. On windy days it is useful to have a few round-headed nails hammered part-way into the bird table tray, so that entire crusts or slices of bread can be speared firmly down and not blown away. In frosty weather, a bird-pudding would be a welcome addition to the menu. Mix food scraps, seeds and peanuts together in a pudding basin. Pour melted fat over the mixture and stir well in. Place in a refrigerator to set before placing it on the bird table for an enthusiastic reception.

Bird-Bath

A pleasantly rustic-looking bird-bath can be made at a very reasonable cost, by placing an earthenware dish about 12" (30 cm.) in diameter and approximately 1" (2.5 cm.) deep, on top of a large log. Dishes like these can be obtained from garden centres, where they are designed to be used beneath conventional flowerpots. Birds need water as much as they need food, even in cold weather, both for drinking purposes and to keep their plumage in good clean condition in order to keep out the cold. Grasses and wild flowers will grow up attractively around the log, and the bird-bath will be high enough to make it awkward for leaping cats.

This type of bird-bath has an advantage over a conventional

design, in that if you keep a duplicate earthenware dish indoors, when the outside one freezes up you can exchange it for the spare dish. If this is not possible, try standing a sink-plunger upright in the centre of your bird-bath in frosty weather. As long as the water is not completely frozen, it should be possible to lift up the plunger by its handle and remove the ice at the same time.

❧ Chapter 14 ❧
Record-keeping

IT'S WELL WORTHWHILE keeping records, and not just for the day when your site becomes famous for a cluster of lady's slipper orchids germinating after a gap of a hundred years. In the more immediate future it's a splendid tonic, when you're recuperating with a cup of hot chocolate after a dose of November flu, to be able to re-read your notes of that sunny day in April, when the willow warbler's melodious song echoed from the topmost twig of your flowering cherry tree.

The main ingredient is a nature notebook, in which any interesting items can be noted down as and when they occur. It may be the arrival of the year's first swallow, a sketch of an extraordinary beetle found in the log pile, or the date of sowing a particular kind of wildflower seeds. The records can be as brief or detailed as you wish, but all will become increasingly useful to refer to as time passes by and more information accumulates to compare and contrast. There is much still to be discovered about even the commonest plants and creatures, and some of it is quite likely to come to light whilst you are sipping an early morning cup of tea and gazing absently at your flowery patch of earth.

Photographs are a great asset for interesting and accurate record-keeping. A video camera too is a possibility for recording memorable moments, such as a family picnic amongst purple knapweed, or hay-making in a heat wave. It is useful to photograph a few sample views on a yearly basis, as well as the seasonal edited highlights, for direct comparisons. This is a great help when you feel nothing has grown—for then you can see that it has. It is a pity that wild rose-coloured spectacles cannot be supplied to wild gardeners, since the greatest temptation to abandon your project comes after the initial work has been completed and you have time to sit back and admire it. Unfortunately, unadulterated nature moves at its own pace, but if you can just survive that hiatus of the initial years, all will be well. Luckily, imagination can expand a single primrose bud into a future flower-laden cushion, and lying beneath a tiny silver birch which has just put forth its first fledgling leaves can produce an optimistic vision of what it will be like to walk beneath this same tree in a few years time, and—amazingly—this does turn out to be true.

For easy reference I also keep yearly lists of flowers, birds, animals, insects and grasses seen in our little meadow. This way, trends are relatively easy to spot. If some species vanish, are we doing something wrong which needs to be corrected, or perhaps this could itself be an advantage—for instance the replacement of coarse grasses with finer ones?

Another type of list is a growth record of average height and girth of our trees. I am a strictly non-mathematical person, but even I enjoy noting down our saplings' vital statistics. Some trees shrink at first, the result of a combination of drought and plump birds perching on the topmost twigs; but eventually most win through and start to stretch towards the sky. Some species grow faster than others: alders and silver birch are particularly quick off the mark. Others, like the oak, are more sedate, but will be standing tall long after the early-starters have fallen to the ground. There is room for them all.

Charts, too, have their place. Our first one was described earlier, when a grid map was drawn up using the fence posts (approximately 9' or 2.7 m. apart) as markers. Within every square the presence of each flower species was noted with a separate symbol; not as tricky a job as it sounds, since each square averaged only four different flower species. Once completed, this chart showed at a glance where the drifts of various plants occurred and, equally usefully, where dull patches predominated. We do not repeat this process every year: only now and then, to see how our flower/grass mix is progressing.

Keeping a chart of our badgers' visiting times is an interesting ongoing occupation. We are only just beginning to see a pattern emerging, but no doubt this will vary from badger to badger as the years go by.

A simple bar chart is useful for totting up monthly rainfall totals. We use a basic graduated tube (available from most garden shops) for our measurements, but it is certainly possible to be much more scientific in weather recording if you wish, perhaps including daily temperatures and wind direction.

Our last record, but probably the most important, is the yearly management plan. In this we note down the year's regular tasks and the months in which they should be carried out. These jobs include loosening tree-ties, haymaking, mulch-spreading for trees and hedges, re-applying preservative to garden furniture, autumn grass-mowing and finally hedge-trimming (remembering to leave a generous helping of berries for the birds). All obvious tasks, I realize, but it wouldn't do to miss them, and anyway it is very satisfying to be able to tick them off when completed.

Meadow Flowers in a Sample Year

Autumn Hawkbit
Betony
Bird's-foot-trefoil
Black Bryony
Black Knapweed
Bluebell
Broad-leaved
   Willowherb
Bugle
Cat's-ear
Cleavers
Common Daisy
Common Field
   Speedwell
Common Orache
Common Vetch
Cow Parsley
Cowslip

Creeping Buttercup
Cuckooflower
   (also known as
   Milkmaid and
   Lady's Smock)
Dandelion
Dock
Dog Rose
Evening Primrose
Fat Hen
Feverfew
Field Garlic
Field Rose
Forget-me-not
Foxglove
Germander
   Speedwell
Goldilocks Buttercup

Great Willowherb
Greater Plantain
Ground Ivy
Groundsel
Hairy Bitter-cress
Hedge Bindweed
Herb-bennet
   (also known as
   Wood Avens)
Herb-Robert
Ivy-leaved Speedwell
Knotgrass
Lesser Celandine
Lesser Stitchwort
Lesser Trefoil
Many-seeded
   Goosefoot
Meadow Buttercup
(continued overleaf)

Meadow Flowers in a Sample Year

(continued)

Meadow Vetchling	Ribwort Plantain	Toadflax
Mouse-ear	Scarlet Pimpernel	Violet
Oxeye Daisy	Scentless Mayweed	White Clover
Pansy	Self-heal	Wild Daffodil
Perennial Sow-thistle	Perforate	Wild Strawberry
Persicaria	St. John's-wort	Wood Anemone
Primrose	Smooth	Woundwort
Ragged Robin	Hawk's-beard	Yarrow
Red Campion	Snowdrop	Yellow Archangel
Red Clover	Sorrel	Yellow Rattle
Red Dead-nettle	Stinging Nettle	

Birds observed in our Meadow in a Sample Year

Blackbird	Grey Heron	Pied Wagtail
Blue Tit	Hedge Sparrow	Robin
Carrion Crow	Herring Gull	Skylark
Chaffinch	House Martin	Song Thrush
Coal Tit	House Sparrow	Stock Dove
Goldfinch	Jackdaw	Swallow
Great Tit	Jay	Swift
Great Spotted	Kestrel	Treecreeper
Woodpecker	Linnet	Willow Warbler
Green	Long-tailed Tit	Wood Pigeon
Woodpecker	Mallard	Wren
Greenfinch	Nuthatch	Yellowhammer

❦ Chapter 15 ❦

Meadow Calendar

JANUARY

❦ If snow falls, look out for animal tracks. Perhaps a fox's straight line of single footprints will converge upon scattered pale-grey breast feathers, which are all that remain of a luckless woodpigeon. Miniature rows of footprints with a tail-line running between them show where tiny creatures have pattered hurriedly along, ever fearful of being pounced upon in this camouflage-free terrain; whilst meandering across a meadow may go the prints (two short—two long, two short—two long) of a lolloping rabbit.

❦ Cold weather may bring unusual birds into closer view, possibly following your regular bird-table customers. Tiny goldcrests forsake the frozen tree-tops to forage on the ground, bramblings may join with flocks of their chaffinch cousins, or an exotic-looking waxwing could arrive from Scandinavia to perch on your berried shrubs, flashing its crest and wax-tipped wings.

❦ Remember to keep bird-table food and water topped up, as your resident birds will have to come to depend on you.

❦ Water meadows act as magnets for flocks of ducks, geese and swans at this time of year.

❦ Small clouds of winter gnats dance in the air on fine afternoons, looking strangely out of season.

❦ Finally, when January just seems to go on far too long, search for the spears of emerging snowdrops, whose gracefully curved white petals will raise your spirits on dismal days.

FEBRUARY

🦋 Robins sing bravely on and off all winter, but the odd sunny day in February will entice other birds such as great tits and mistle thrushes into experimental bursts of song.

🦋 Flocks of greenfinches 'wheeze' from the bushes. They are too plump to squeeze through the outer squirrel-proof bars of peanut dispensers, but have learnt to lean in and peck at the nuts successfully.

🦋 Snipe feed hungrily in water meadows, probing the soft mud with their long bills.

🦋 Flies may well emerge from hibernation on days like these, but they are likely to regret it before long.

🦋 The first primroses smile upwards from their leafy nests.

🦋 Hazel catkins unravel their yellow-pollened tassels to flutter bravely in the breeze. Their country name of 'lambstails' seems particularly apt now, bringing to mind the quivers of delight in the tail of a new-born lamb which is suckling milk from its mother.

🦋 Goat willow branches are buttoned with silver and gold downy catkins, making its folk name of 'pussy willow' most appropriate.

🦋 Badger cubs are born safe and snug into their warm hay-lined setts beneath the ground.

🦋 The earth draws breath from its battle with winter, and so do we.

MARCH

❧ The chaffinch gives full voice to his passionate spring song, amongst the unfurling leaves of a hornbeam tree. Indeed, the dawn chorus increases in volume and diversity every morning: romance and optimism for the coming year are in the air.

❧ Primroses are in their element at this time of year, their fragile beauty seemingly indifferent to wind and rain.

❧ Violets are in flower, within the shelter of their parasol of leaves. Dog violets display a proliferation of tiny mauve blooms, while the gentle fragrance of sweet violets is a balm in today's hurried world.

❧ Golden celandines star pathways and hedge-banks. Colt's-foot is another early flower, with fleshy scale-like leaves and similarly well-insulated yellow flower buds.

❧ Frogs and toads head for ponds—often those in gardens, now that farm and village ponds are hard to come by—in order to lay their spawn. Dollops of frogs spawn jelly are familiar from childhood days, whilst toads spawn appears in long strands. In either case, each black dot should change into a comma shape, then become a free-swimming tadpole, soon to grow legs. Eventually the survivors emerge from their watery nursery, ready to explore the wider world.

❧ Time to dust off the strimmer ready to cut the grass paths on odd occasions between now and September.

APRIL

🦋 Early Brimstone and Small Tortoise-shell butterflies emerge still dazed from their hibernation, to flutter haphazardly about.

🦋 Hedgehogs also emerge from hibernation, eager for a meal of succulent slugs.

🦋 Migrant birds arrive from warmer climates, including those two species that look so alike yet sing so differently: the chiffchaff and willow warbler. Most welcome of all is the swallow, trailing in its wake the promise of sunny days to come.

🦋 Song thrushes begin building mud-lined grassy nests, while for extra comfort blackbirds add an inner layer of soft grasses to theirs.

🦋 Ice-pure white blossom shines from the leafless branches of blackthorn bushes.

🦋 There is a flash of warmer colour, though, as a jay flies past, giving its harsh alarm cry like the ripping of an old sheet.

🦋 Water meadows gleam with rich clusters of kingcups (marsh marigolds).

🦋 Meadow fox-tail and sweet vernal-grass begin to lengthen, and amongst them wild daffodils pit their wits against the strong breeze.

🦋 Clusters of blackfly pounce on succulent new plant buds, shortly to be joined by ladybirds—which pounce on the blackfly.

🦋 Now is the time to loosen tree-ties to take account of the sudden upsurge in growth.

MAY

❧ A lovely month, when bluebells flood the woodland floor and cowslips infiltrate the meadows.

❧ Cuckoos call by day from the newly leafed tree-tops, and with luck a nightingale sings from the bushes by night.

❧ Swifts zoom over the meadows, shouting with exhilaration—as would I if only I could fly like that.

❧ Closer to earth, things are equally busy, with queen bumblebees choosing nest sites beneath clumps of dead grass or leaves, or down a convenient mousehole.

❧ Buttercups, oxeye daisies and pink sorrel bloom ever more profusely as the month progresses.

❧ Damp field corners are brightened by the hazy pink and mauve flower clusters of milkmaids (cuckoo-flowers).

❧ Hawthorn blossom froths creamy-white amongst the fresh greenery. As hawthorn is the preferred food plant of so many different types of moth caterpillars, it is a wonder that any leaves are left, and yet it is one of our most prolific hedge plants.

❧ If there is a stream nearby, the breeze carries with it the tang of wild garlic (ramsons), with their white spiky galaxies of flowers and aromatic leaves.

❧ Should the stream deepen to become a river, a kingfisher may be glimpsed as it flashes by, heading for its nest-hole excavated in the riverbank.

❧ On warm evenings, badger cubs venture out for carefree play around their sett entrance.

JUNE

🌺 On the practical side, this is a good time to check your fences are steady.

🌺 Young blue tits leave the safety of their nest boxes and fly to nearby treetops. They travel in family groups, squeaking constantly to keep in touch with each other.

🌺 Turtle doves croon drowsily of an afternoon.

🌺 Mixed flocks of finches munch their way through meadows, erupting in a twittering cloud when anyone strolls past.

🌺 The lopsidedly curving blue plumes of tufted vetch flaunt themselves along the hedgerows.

🌺 Honeysuckle drapes the hedgerows and tiny wild strawberries offer a deliciously sweet snack.

🌺 The seeds of yellow rattle do indeed rattle inside their seed pods, like a child's toy.

🌺 Meadow flowers vie with grasses in the race to bloom and set their seeds for next year.

🌺 Meadow Brown butterflies home in on their natural environment.

🌺 In water meadows, yellow flag irises attract enthusiastic hoverflies, while on drier ground bird's-foot-trefoil is also a magnet for humming insects.

🌺 Fox cubs can sometimes be seen at play, their auburn fur glinting in the sunshine as they pounce on imaginary foes.

JULY

❦ In dry meadows, delicate china-blue harebells tremble in the slightest breeze on their thread-like stems. Pink mallow also blossoms, in a perfect colour contrast.

❦ Wild roses are rampant now that summer has really arrived, with arching sprays of delicately-scented flowers shading from blush-cream to vermilion.

❦ The tall foxglove spires also bloom flamboyantly, and bees spend a great deal of time buzzing in a muffled fashion from inside their flower bells.

❦ Ringlets and Gatekeepers join the butterfly clan.

❦ Grasshoppers zither busily in meadows (crickets, although similar in appearance, generally have much longer antennae than grasshoppers).

❦ Green shield bugs (so-named because their shape resembles a mediæval knight's shield) can often be seen seemingly idling their time away on leaves.

❦ On warm afternoons black ants swarm in nuptial flights—many being elegantly caught and eaten in mid-air by swifts, swallows and house martens, not forgetting the humble house sparrow.

❦ Bats are kept busy of an evening hawking for insects.

❦ This month's main task is to mow, dry and gather the hay, be it for animal fodder or the compost heap. A tiring job, but just think of all the energy saved by not having had to mow it until now; and there's a great sense of achievement afterwards.

AUGUST

❧ Time to enjoy sunbathing in your newly-mown meadow.

❧ Birds and animals too seem exhausted by the heat, leaving insects alone to enjoy a field day—fluttering, crawling and sleepily humming the hours away—so it is an opportunity to admire the shimmering beauty of darting dragonflies and damselflies.

❧ Each tall teasel sports a mauve ruff, extending daily by degrees over every spiny seedhead, a delight for bees, and later for finches.

❧ Apparently unaffected by drought, purple knapweed flowers steadily.

❧ Meadows with a river running by are fringed with garlands of purple loosestrife and aromatic water-mint.

❧ On chalk downland, anthills in ancient meadows mimic in miniature the nearby prehistoric earthworks and burial mounds. Such hummocks have their own specific flora, often including thyme and eyebright.

❧ Regularly, at around 8 o'clock in the evening, the plump buds of evening primroses open on their tall stems as a tempting invitation to passing moths.

❧ Roe deer can be spotted more easily in meadows of an evening or early morning now, distinguished by their neatly pronged antlers and light rump patches—visible when they bound away.

❧ In more energetic moments, consider erecting nestboxes, giving time for them to be readily accepted by birds for roosting and nesting.

SEPTEMBER

🌿 Early morning dew-drops sparkle on spiders webs, meriting a second glance from even those people most eager to dash past.

🌿 Flowers and fruit mingle on the blackberry bushes, attracting Comma and Red Admiral butterflies—not to mention hungry humans.

🌿 The green flowers of ivy provide a welcome source of nectar for insects just now.

🌿 Chillier temperatures prompt the annual application of preservative to garden furniture.

🌿 Flocks of swallows congregate at this time of year, pegging themselves onto telegraph wires and twittering as excitedly as passengers in any airport departure lounge. How sad it is to see them go.

🌿 Time to check the tree-ties again, to ensure that they are not throttling the saplings they are intended to help support.

🌿 Trim hedges, remembering to leave plenty of berries for birds and small mammals in the coming winter. If you have access to both sides of a hedge, aim for the base to be wider than the top, thus producing an A-shape.

🌿 If you wish to sow wild flowers in plain grassy areas, dig up patches, sprinkle the seeds, firm them down and then water in.

OCTOBER

❧ Trees are laden with plump nuts and richly shining berries, all of which the local animals and birds are keen to sample.

❧ Animals eat hazel nuts in differing ways: wood mice leave a corrugated hole in the shell with teeth marks around the outside; dormice nibble a tidy polished hole with the addition of a prominent outer ring of teeth marks; bank voles simply cut neat holes; and squirrels prize nuts open from an end.

❧ Squirrels and jays bury their surplus acorns, forgetting many—and thus planting many a potential giant oak.

❧ Tree and hedgerow leaves clamour for attention, changing their uniform green colour to bright mixtures of yellow, orange, russet and scarlet.

❧ Fascinating fungi pop up unpredictably, ranging from tiny fairy rings to giant puffballs.

❧ October sees the time for a meadow's autumn cut (unless you have had animals grazing on it), after which the relatively short cuttings can be use for mulch or added to compost.

❧ If you have the chance, top up your log pile (which will have rotted away somewhat over the past year) to give added cover for insects and small animals in the harsh weather to come.

NOVEMBER

❧ Beech hedges take on a bronze hue, while other leaves are tumbled to the ground by strong winds and lashing rain. There are exceptions, like silver birches, whose shield-shaped leaves are now golden, making the trees resemble over-decorated school prefects.

❧ Hazel trees may be coppiced now that the sap is no longer rising.

❧ Red deadnettle may still be blooming bravely in a sheltered corner.

❧ November is a good month to spot previously unsuspected birds' nests in the now bare branches of trees and hedges, varying from a long-tailed tit's nest (a miraculous tiny dome of moss and feathers), to a magpie's vast domed edifice topped with apparently clumsily placed twigs.

❧ Bedraggled blue and great tits peck at peanuts on the birdtable, their feathers blown up at uncomfortable punk-like angles.

❧ Large flocks of starlings fly by on triangular wings, chattering as they swing across the sunset sky, heading for their communal roost.

❧ Finally, at dusk, a little owl may be seen perched, upright as a guardsman, on the end of a dead tree branch.

DECEMBER

❧ A robin poses plumply on the birdtable, hinting that Christmas should include extra helpings of cake crumbs.

❧ If you are lucky enough to have a local gorse bush it will probably still sport a few golden flowers, for as the proverb goes, 'when the gorse is out of bloom, then kissing's out of tune'—in other words, never!

❧ Distant ash trees are tall and gaunt against a leaden sky. One morning you may awake to find every hedgerow twig and sapling bough encased in the milky white armour of a hoarfrost.

❧ Fieldfares and redwings blow in on the north wind. Try imitating their "tut-tut-tut" call by sucking your teeth loudly, for they may fly towards you.

❧ Try attracting curious woodpeckers by tapping a pebble sharply three or four times against a tree trunk.

❧ It is useful to clean out nestboxes so that parasites do not become a problem.

❧ Vole nest-holes show clearly in wind-flattened grassy banks; some owners are clearly better housekeepers than others and pull dead leaves snugly into the entrances to stop the draught.

❧ In Scotland, stoats will moult into their white winter coats, leaving only their black tail-tips as contrast.

❧ The eerie cries of a vixen seeking a mate echo into the starlit night.

Time to look forward to spring.

Lists of Species: British Isles

MEADOW FLOWERS

Key: A = acid soil; N = neutral soil
C = calcareous soil; W = prefers damp conditions

Achillea spp. (inc. Sneezewort + Yarrow)	ANC
Agrimony (*Agrimonia eupatoria*)	NC
Angelica (*Angelica sylvestris*)	NCW
Bartsia / Odontites spp.	ANC
Bedstraw (*Galium* spp.)	ANC
Bird's-foot-trefoil (*Lotus corniculatus*)	NC
Bugle (*Ajuga* spp.)	NC
Burnet Saxifrage (*Pimpinella saxifraga*)	NC
Buttercup (*Ranunculus* spp.)	NC
Campanula spp. (inc. Harebell + Bellflowers)	ANC
Campion (*Silene* spp.)	NC
Cat's-ear (*Hypochoeris* spp.)	NC
Cinquefoil (*Potentilla* spp.)	ANC
Clary (*Salvia* spp.)	NC
Clover (*Trifolium* spp.)	ANC
Comfrey (*Symphytum officinale*)	NCW
Cow Parsley (*Anthriscus sylvestris*)	NC
Cranesbill (*Geranium* spp.)	ANC
Cuckoo-flower (*Cardamine pratensis*)	NCW
Daffodil (*Narcissus* spp.)	ANC
Daisy (*Bellis perennis*)	ANC
Dandelion (*Taraxacum* spp.)	NC
Dead-nettle (*Lamium* spp.)	ANC
Dyer's Greenweed (*Genista tinctoria*)	AN
Evening Primrose (*Oenothera biennis*)	ANC
Eyebright (*Euphrasia* spp.)	ANC
Fleabane (*Erigeron* spp.)	N
Forget-me-not (*Myosotis* spp.)	ANC
Fumitory (*Fumaria* spp.)	ANC
Great Burnet (*Sanguisorba officinalis*)	NCW
Hawksbeard (*Crepis* spp.)	ANC
Hawkbit (*Leontodon* spp.)	NC
Hawkweed (*Hieracium / Pilosella* spp.)	ANC

Himalayan Balsam (*Impatiens glandulifera*)	NCW
Iris spp.	NCW
Kidney Vetch (*Anthyllis vulneraria*)	C
Knapweed (*Centaurea* spp.)	ANC
Lathyrus spp. (inc. Meadow Vetchling)	ANC
Lysimachia spp. (inc. Creeping Jenny)	NCW
Mallow (*Malva* spp.)	ANC
Marjoram (*Origanum vulgare*)	C
Marsh marigold (*Caltha palustris*)	NCW
Meadow-rue (*Thalictrum* spp.)	NCW
Meadowsweet (*Filipendula ulmaria*)	NCW
Milkwort (*Polygala* spp.)	ANC
Mint (*Mentha* spp.)	ANCW
Mouse-ear (*Cerastium* spp.)	NC
Orchid family (Orchidaceae)	ANC
Oxeye Daisy (*Chrysanthemum leucanthemum* / *Leucanthemum vulgare*)	
	NC
Pepper saxifrage (*Silaum silaus*)	ANCW
Phyteuma spp. (inc. Rampions)	C
Plantain (*Plantago* spp.)	ANC
Primula spp. (inc. Primrose + Cowslip)	ANC
Purple Loosestrife (*Lythrum salicaria*)	NCW
Ragged-Robin (*Lychnis flos-cuculi*)	NCW
Restharrow (*Ononis repens*)	NC
St. John's Wort (*Hypericum* spp.)	ANC
Salad Burnet (*Poterium sanguisorba*)	C
Saxifrage (*Saxifraga* spp.)	NC
Scabious (*Scabiosa* / *Knautia* spp.)	ANC
Selfheal (*Prunella vulgaris*)	ANC
Skullcap (*Scutellaria galericulata*)	ANCW
Soapwort (*Saponaria officinalis*)	NC
Sorrel (*Rumex* spp.)	ANC
Speedwell (*Veronica* spp.)	ANC
Stitchwort (*Stellaria* spp.)	AN
Tansy (*Chrysanthemum* / *Tanacetum vulgare*)	ANC
Teasel (*Dipsacus* spp.)	NC
Thyme (*Thymus* spp.)	ANC
Toadflax (*Linaria* spp.)	NC
Trefoil (*Trifolium* spp.)	NC
Vetch (*Vicia* spp.)	NC
Violet (*Viola* spp.)	ANC
Water-pepper (*Polygonum hydropiperoides*)	ANCW
Watercress (*Nasturtium officinale* / *Rorippa nasturtium-aquaticum*)	NCW
Wild Basil (*Clinopodium vulgare*)	C

Wild Carrot (*Daucus carota*)	NC
Wild Parsnip (*Pastinaca sativa*)	C
Willowherb (*Epilobium* spp.)	ANC
Woundwort (*Stachys* spp.)	ANC

MEADOW GRASSES

Cocksfoot (*Dactylis glomerata*)	NC
Common Bent (*Agrostis capillaris*)	ANC
Common Quaking-grass (*Briza media*)	CN
Creeping Bent (*Agrostis stolonifera*)	N
Creeping Soft-grass (*Holcus mollis*)	AN, Shady
Crested Dog's-tail (*Cynosurus cristatus*)	ANC
Downy Oat-grass (*Helictotrichon pubescens*)	CN
False Oat-grass (*Arrhenatherum elatius*)	NC
Giant Fescue (*Festuca gigantea*)	Shady
Hairy Brome (*Bromus ramosus*)	WN
Meadow Fox-tail (*Alopecurus pratensis*)	WN
Red Fescue (*Festuca rubra*)	CN
Reed Canary-grass (*Phalaris arundinacea*)	WN
Rough Meadow-grass (*Poa trivialis*)	N
Rye (*Lolium perenne*)	N
Smooth Meadow-grass (N. America: Kentucky Bluegrass) (*Poa pratensis*)	N
Sweet Vernal-grass (*Anthoxanthum odoratum*)	AC
Timothy (*Phleum pratense*)	N
Tor (*Brachypodium pinnatum*)	C
Tufted Hair-grass (*Deschampsia caespitosa*)	NCW, Shady
Wall Barley (*Hordeum murinum*)	N
Yellow / Golden Oat-grass (*Trisetum flavescens*)	C
Yorkshire Fog (N. America: Velvet Grass) (*Holcus lanatus*)	NC

TREES & SHRUBS

Strong preferences as regards soil types are given below.

Aspen (*Populus tremula*)	
Beech (*Fagus sylvatica*)	
Bird Cherry (*Prunus padus*)	W
Black Poplar (*Populus nigra*)	C
Blackthorn (*Prunus spinosa*)	
Box (*Buxus sempervirens*)	C

Common Alder (*Alnus glutinosa*)	WC
Common Ash (*Fraxinus excelsior*)	
Common Hazel (*Corylus avellana*)	C
Common Pear (*Pyrus communis*)	
Common Yew (*Taxus baccata*)	C
Crab Apple (*Malus sylvestris*)	C
Crack Willow (*Salix fragilis*)	W
Elder (*Sambucus nigra*)	C
English Elm (*Ulmus procera*)	
Field Maple (*Acer campestre*)	C
Goat Willow, also known as Pussy Willow (*Salix caprea*)	W
Guelder-rose (*Viburnum opulus*)	WC
Hawthorn (*Crataegus monogyna*)	
Holly (*Ilex aquifolium*)	
Hornbeam (*Carpinus betulus*)	C
Horse Chestnut (*Aesculus hippocastanum*)	
Juniper (*Juniperus communis*)	
Osier (*Salix viminalis*)	W
Pedunculate / English Oak (*Quercus pendunculata / robur*)	C
Rowan (*Sorbus aucuparia*)	A
Scots Pine (*Pinus sylvestris*)	A
Sea-buckthorn (*Hippophae rhamnoides*)	
Sessile / Durmast Oak (*Quercus petraea*)	
Silver Birch (N. America: European White Birch) (*Betula pendula*)	A
Small-leafed Lime (*Tilia cordata*)	C
Spindle (*Euonymus europaea*)	
White Willow (*Salix alba*)	W
Whitebeam (*Sorbus aria*)	C
Wild Cherry (*Prunus avium*)	A
Wild Pear (*Pyrus communis*)	
Wild Service Tree (*Sorbus torminalis*)	C
Wych Elm (*Ulmus glabra*)	

MEADOW BUTTERFLIES

together with the food plants preferred by their caterpillars.

Adonis Blue (*Lysandra bellargus*)	Vetch
Brimstone (*Gonepteryx rhamni*)	Buckthorn
Brown Argus (*Aricia agestis*)	Rock-rose
Chalk-hill Blue (*Lysandra coridon*)	Vetch
Chequered Skipper (*Carterocephalus palaemon*)	Grass
Clouded Yellow (*Colias crocea*)	Clover

Comma (*Polygonia c, album*)	Nettle
Common Blue (*Polyommatus icarus*)	Vetch
Dark Green Fritillary (*Mesoacidalia aglaja*)	Violet
Dingy Skipper (*Erynnis tages*)	Trefoil
Essex Skipper (*Thymelicus lineola*)	Grass
Gatekeeper (*Pyronia tithonus*)	Grass
Grayling (*Hipparchia semele*)	Grass
Green-veined White (*Pieris napi*)	Crucifers
Grizzled Skipper (*Pyrgus centaureae*)	Mallow
Large Skipper (*Ochlodes venatus*)	Grass
Large White (*Pieris brassicae*)	Cabbage
Little (or Small) Blue (*Cupido minimus*)	Vetch
Marbled White (*Melanargia galathea*)	Grass
Marsh Fritillary (*Euphydryas aurinia*)	Devil's-bit Scabious
Meadow Brown (*Maniola jurtina*)	Grass
Mountain Argus (*Aricia allous*)	Rock-rose
Orange-tip (*Anthocharis cardamines*)	Crucifers
Painted Lady (*Vanessa cardui*)	Thistle
Peacock (*Inachis io*)	Nettle
Red Admiral (*Vanessa atalanta*)	Nettle
Ringlet (*Coenonympha tullia*)	Grass
Silver-spotted Skipper (*Epargyreus clarus*)	Grass
Small Copper (*Lycaena phlaeas*)	Dock/Sorrel
Small Heath (*Ceonymphus pamphilus*)	Grass
Small Skipper (*Thymelicus sylvestris*)	Grass
Small Tortoise-shell (*Aglais urticae*)	Nettle
Small White (*Pieris rapae*)	Cabbage
Swallowtail (*Papilio machaon britannicus*)	Umbellifers
Wall Brown (*Lasiommata megera*)	Grass

Lists of Species: North America

MEADOW FLOWERS

Key: A = acid soil; N = neutral soil; C = calcareous (alkaline) soil
D = drought-tolerant; W = prefers or tolerates wet conditions

Alexander (*Zizia aptera* and *Z. aurea*)	WD
Aster (*Aster* spp.)	WD
Baby's Breath (*Gypsophila paniculata*)	C
Beardtongue (*Penstemon* spp.)	D
Bee Balm/Bergamot (*Monarda* spp.)	DW
Bird's-foot Violet (*Viola pedata*)	
Bishop's Weed (*Ammi majus*)	
Black-eyed Susan (*Rudbeckia hirta*)	D
Blackberry Lily (*Belamcanda chinensis*)	
Blackfoot Daisy (*Melanpodium leucanthum*)	N
Blanketflower (*Gaillardia aristata*)	
Blazing-star/Gayfeather (*Liatris* spp.)	WD
Blue-eyed Grass (*Sisyrinchium* spp.)	
Bouncing Bet (*Saponaria officinalis*)	
Butterfly Weed (*Asclepias tuberosa*)	AD
California Poppy (*Eschscholzia californica* and other spp.)	
Camass (*Camassia* spp.)	W
Carpet Bugle (*Ajuga reptans*)	
Compass Plant (*Silphium laciniatum*)	W
Coreopsis (*Coreopsis lanceolata* and other spp.)	CD
Culver's Root (*Veronicastrum virginicum*)	W
Dame's Rocket (*Hesperis matronalis*)	
Dwarf Crested Iris (*Iris cristata*)	C
Eastern Columbine (*Aquilegia canadensis*)	
Evening Primrose (*Oenothera* spp.)	D
False Chamomile (*Boltonia asteroides*)	
False Indigo (*Baptisia* spp.)	AW
False Lupine (*Thermopsis montana*)	W
Fireweed (*Epilobium angustifolium*)	WD
Goldenrod (*Solidago* spp.)	D
Gooseneck Loosestrife (*Lysimachia clethroides*)	W
Great Blue Lobelia (*Lobelia siphilitica*)	W
Harebell (*Campanula rotundifolia*)	D
Indian Paintbrush (*Castilleja* spp.)	

Ironweed (*Vernonia* spp.)	W
Joe-Pye Weed (*Eupatorium purpureum*)	W
Johnny-jump-up / Wild Pansy (*Viola tricolor*)	
Jupiter's Beard (*Centranthus ruber*)	
Leadplant (*Amorpha canescens*)	D
Meadow Rue (*Thalictrum polygamum*)	
Mexican Hat (*Ratibida columnifera*)	
Milkweed (*Asclepias syriaca* and other spp.)	W
Mountain Mint (*Pycnanthemum* spp.)	
Mullein (*Verbascum thapsus*)	D
Nodding Onion (*Allium cernuum*)	WDA
Obedient Plant (*Physiostega virginiana*)	
Oxeye Daisy (*Chrysanthemum leucanthemum*)	A
Partridge Pea (*Cassia fasciculata*)	
Pearly Everlasting (*Anaphalis margaritacea*)	
Perovskia/Russian Sage (*Perovskia atriplicifolia*)	C
Prairie Clover (*Dalea/Petalostemon* spp.)	WD
Prairie Smoke (*Geum triflorum*)	CD
Purple Coneflower (*Echinacea* spp.)	
Queen-of-the-prairie (*Filipendula rubra*)	W
Rattlesnake-master (*Eryngium yuccifolium*)	C
Sage (*Salvia* spp.)	CDW
Shooting-star (*Dodecatheon* spp.)	
Sneezeweed (*Helenium autumnale*)	W
Spiderwort (*Tradescentia virginiana*)	
Sulfur Flower (*Eriogonum umbellatum*)	D
Sunflower (*Helianthus* spp.)	
Tawny (or Orange) Daylily (*Hemerocallis fulva*)	
Texas Bluebonnet (*Lupinus texensis*)	
Turk's-cap Lily (*Lilium superbum*)	WA
Turtlehead (*Chelone glabra*)	W
Viper's Bugloss (*Echium vulgare*)	C
Western Blue Flag (*Iris missouriensis*)	WC
Wild Blue (or Prairie) Flax (*Linum perenne var. lewisii*)	W
Wild Geranium (*Geranium maculatum*)	W
Wild Lupine (*Lupinus perennis*)	A
Wild Strawberry (*Fragaria virginiana*)	
Yarrow (*Achillea millefolium* and other spp.)	D
Yellow Coneflower (*Ratibida pinnata*)	NDW

MEADOW GRASSES

Alkali Dropseed (*Sporobolus airoides*)	WD
Big Bluestem (*Andropogon gerardii*)	D
Blue Grama (*Bouteloua gracilis*)	D
Blue Fescue (*Festuca ovina* var. *glauca*)	
Blue Moor Grass (*Sesleria caerulea/S. autumnalis*)	C
Blue Wild Rye (*Elymus glaucus*)	
Broomsedge (*Andropogon virginicus*)	
Buffalo Grass (*Buchloe dactyloides*)	D
Bulbous Oat Grass (*Arrhenatherum elatius* var. *bulbosum*)	
Bushy Bluestem (*Andropogon glomeratus*)	W
California Fescue (*Festuca californica*)	
California Meadow Sedge (*Carex pansa*)	
Canada Wild Rye (*Elymus canadensis*)	D
Cotton Grass (*Eriophorum vaginatum*)	AW
Deergrass (*Muhlenbergia rigens*)	D
Feather Reedgrass (*Calamagrostis acutifolia* var. *stricta*)	W
Fine-Leaved Fescue (*Festuca tenuifolia*)	
Foothill Sedge (*Carex tumulicola*)	WD
Foxtail Barley (*Hordeum jubatum*)	
Indian Rice Grass (*Oryzopsis hymenoides*)	D
Indian Grass (*Sorghastrum nutans*)	D
Junegrass (*Koeleria cristata*)	D
Leafy Reed Grass (*Calamagrostis foliosa*)	
Little Bluestem (*Schizachyrium scoparium*)	D
Meadow Foxtail (*Alopecurus pratensis*)	
Needle-and-thread Grass (*Stipa comata*)	
Northern (Prairie) Dropseed (*Sporobolus heterolepis*)	D
Orchard Grass (*Dactylis glomerata*)	
Prairie Cordgrass (*Spartina pectinata*)	W
Purple Lovegrass (*Eragrostis spectabilis*)	D
Purple Top (*Tridens flavus*)	
Red Fescue (*Festuca rubra*)	
Sideoats Grama (*Bouteloua curtipendula*)	D
Silver Beardgrass (*Andropogon ternarius*)	D
Sweet Vernal Grass (*Anthoxanthum odoratum*)	AW
Switchgrass (*Panicum virgatum*)	WD
Tufted Hair Grass (*Deschampsia caespitosa*)	D
Velvet Grass (*Holcus lanatus*)	
Western Wheatgrass (*Agropyron smithii*)	
Wild Oats (*Chasmanthium latifolium*)	W
Wiregrass (*Aristida stricta*)	D

TREES & SHRUBS

Strong preferences as regards soil types are given below.

American Beech (*Fagus grandiflora*)	
American Mountain Ash (*Sorbus americana*)	A
American Persimmon (*Diospyros virginiana*)	
American Wild Plum (*Prunus americana*)	
Bald Cypress (*Taxodium distichum*)	W
Birch (*Betula* spp.)	
Black Ash (*Fraxinus nigra*)	W
Black Walnut (*Juglans nigra*)	
Blueberry (*Vaccinium* spp.)	A
Bur Oak (*Quercus macrocarpa*)	A
Butterfly Bush (*Buddleia davidii*)	
Chokecherry (*Prunus virginiana*)	
Common Lilac (*Syringa vulgaris*)	
Cornelian Cherry (*Cornus mas*)	
Crabapple (*Malus* spp.)	
Eastern Red Cedar (*Juniperus virginiana*)	C
Elaeagnus (*Elaeagnus* spp., inc. Russian and autumn olive)	D
Elderberry (*Sambucus canadensis*)	
Flowering Dogwood (*Cornus florida*)	
Feltleaf Ceanothus (*Ceanothus arboreus*)	D
Franklin Tree (*Franklinia alatamaha*)	A
Hawthorn (*Crataegus* spp.)	
Hazelnut (*Corylus* spp.)	
Honey Locust (*Gleditsia triacanthos*)	
Honey Mesquite (*Prosopis glandulosa* var. *glandulosa*)	
Ironwood (*Olneya tesota*)	D
Labrador Tea (*Ledum groenlandicum*)	A
Mulberry (*Morus* spp.)	
New Jersey Tea (*Ceanothus americanus*)	A
Oregon Grape-Holly (*Mahonia aquifolium*)	C
Pasture Rose (*Rosa carolina*)	
Pawpaw (*Asimina triloba*)	
Pine (*Pinus* spp.)	A
Quaking Aspen (*Populus tremuloides*)	
Red Osier Dogwood (*Cornus sericea*)	
Redbud (*Cercis canadensis*)	
Sea Buckthorn (*Hippophae rhamnoides*)	
Serviceberry (*Amelanchier* spp.)	
Shellbark Hickory (*Carya laciniosa*)	A
Silver Maple (*Acer saccharium*)	D

Southern Live Oak (*Quercus virginiana*)	A
Sugar Maple (*Acer saccharum*)	
Sumac (*Rhus* spp.)	
Valley Cottonwood (*Populus fremontii*)	
Viburnum (*Viburnum* spp., inc. American highbush cranberry)	
Witch Hazel (*Hamamelis virginiana*)	
Winterberry (*Ilex verticillata*)	W

MEADOW BUTTERFLIES

together with the food plants preferred by their caterpillars.

American Painted Lady (*Vanessa virginiensis*)	Everlasting
Baltimore (*Euphydras phaeton*)	Turtlehead
Black Swallowtail (*Papilio polyxenes*)	Umbellifers
Blazing-Star Skipper (*Hesperia leonardus*)	Grass
Buckeye (*Junonia coenia*)	Plantain
Checkered Skipper (*Pyrgus communis*)	Mallow
Checkered White (*Pieris protodice*)	Crucifers
Comma (*Polygonia comma*)	Nettle/Hops
Common Sooty Wing (*Pholisora catullus*)	Amaranth
Common Sulphur (*Colias philodice*)	Clover/Vetch
Eastern Tailed Blue (*Everas comyntas*)	Clover/Vetch
European Skipperling (*Thymelicus lineola*)	Grass
Fiery Skipper (*Hylephila phyleus*)	Grass
Fire-Rim Tortoise-shell (*Nymphalis milberti*)	Nettle
Gray Skipper (*Lerodea eufala*)	Grass
Gray Hairstreak (*Strymon melinus*)	Clover/Vetch/Mallow
Great Spangled Fritillary (*Speyeria cybele*)	Violet
Greenish Clover Blue (*Plebejus saepiolus*)	Clover
Holarctic Grass Skipper (*Hesperia comma*)	Grass
Long Dash (*Polites mystic*)	Grass
Meadow Fritillary (*Boloria bellona*)	Violet
Monarch (*Danaus plexippus*)	Milkweed
Orange Sulphur (*Colias eurytheme*)	Clover/Vetch
Painted Lady (*Vanessa cardui*)	Thistle/Knapweed
Peak White (*Pieris callidice*)	Crucifers
Pearl Crescent (*Phyciodes tharos*)	Aster
Prairie Skipper (*Hesperia ottoe*)	Grass
Question Mark (*Polygonia interrogationis*)	Nettle
Red Admiral (*Vanessa atalanta*)	Nettle
Ringlet (*Coenonympha tullia*)	Grass
Sachem (*Atalopedes campestris*)	Grass

Silver Meadow Fritillary (*Boloria selene*)	Violet
Silver-Spotted Skipper (*Epargyreus clarus*)	Legumes
Small White (*Pieris rapae*)	Crucifers
Spring Azure (*Celestrina ladon*)	Dogwood
Viceroy (*Limenitis archippus*)	Willow
Wood Nymph (*Cercyonis pegala*)	Grass

Useful Addresses: Britain

Wildflower Seeds, Bulbs & Plants

British Wild Flower Plants, 23 Yarmouth Road, Ormesby St. Margaret,
Great Yarmouth, NR29 3QE. Includes coastal plants.

Countryside Wildflowers, Somersham, Cambridgeshire, PE17 3DN.

Emorsgate Seeds, Tilney All Saints, Kings Lynn, Norfolk, PE34 4RT.

Landlife, The Old Police Station, Lark Lane, Liverpool, L17 8UU.

The Organic Gardening Catalogue, River Dene Estate, Molesey Road,
Hersham, Surrey KT12 4RG.

Mike Handyside Flowers, 28 Woodlands Park, Allostock, Knutsford,
Cheshire, WA16 9LG.

Really Wild Flowers, H.V. Horticulture Ltd., The Shop, The Street, Sutton
Waldron, Blandford Forum, Dorset, DT11 8NZ.

Native Trees

Most local plant nurseries should be able to supply native trees and
hedges, but in case of difficulty the following nurseries also offer a
mail order service:

England

Buckinghamshire: Buckingham Nurseries & Garden Centre,
14 Tingewick Road, Buckingham MK18 4AE.

Cumbria: Beechcroft Nurseries, Bongate, Appleby CA16 6UE.

Devon: Greenway Gardens, Churston Ferrers, Brixham TQ5 0ES.

Hampshire: Hillier Nurseries Ltd., Ampfield House, Ampfield,
Romsey SO5 9PA.

Kent: Madrona Nursery, Harden Road, Lydd TN29 9LT.
Starborough Nursery, Starborough Road, Marsh Green,
Edenbridge TN8 5RB.
J. Toms Ltd (tree tie specialists), Grigg Lane, Headcorn,
Ashford TN27 9SH

Leicestershire: Goscote Nurseries Ltd., Syston Road, Cossington LE7 4UZ.

Shropshire: Fron Nursery, Fron Issa, Rhewlas, Oswestry SY10 7JH.

Somerset: YSJ Seeds, Kingsfield Conservation Nursery, Broadenham Lane,
Winsham, Chard TA20 4JF.

Scotts Nurseries (Merriott) Ltd, Merriott TA16 5PL.
Suffolk: Notcutts Nurseries, Woodbridge IP12 4AF.
Sussex: English Woodlands, Burrow Nursery, Herrings Lane,
    Cross-in-Hand, Heathfield, East Sussex TN21 0UG.
Wiltshire: Landford Trees, Landford Lodge, Landford, Salisbury SP5 2EH.

Northern Ireland
Daisy Hill Nurseries Ltd., Hospital Road, Newry, County Down BT35 8PN.

Scotland
Earthward, Tweed Horizons, Newtown St. Boswells, Melrose,
    Roxburghshire TD6 0SG.
Ben Reid & Co., Pinewood Park Nurseries, Countesswells Road,
    Aberdeen, Grampian AB9 2QL.

Wales
Waterwheel Nursery, Bully Hole Bottom, Usk Road, Shirenewton,
    Chepstow, Gwent NP6 6SA.

Conservation Organisations

Agroforestry Research Trust, 46 Hunter's Moon, Dartington, Totnes,
    Devon TQ9 6JT.
Landlife, The National Wildflower Centre, Court Hey Park, Liverpool
    L16 3NA.
Flora Locale, 36 Kingfisher Court, Hambridge Road, Newbury, Berkshire
    RG14 5SJ.
Plantlife, The Natural History Museum, Cromwell Road, London SW7 5BD.
Royal Society for the Protection of Birds, (RSPB), The Lodge, Sandy,
    Bedfordshire SG19 2DL.
Woodland Trust, Autumn Park, Dysart Road, Grantham, Lincolnshire
    NG31 6LL.
Friends of the Earth, (FOE), 26-28 Underwood Street, London N1 7JQ.
British Trust for Conservation Volunteers (BTCV), 36 St. Mary's Street,
    Wallingford, Oxfordshire OX10 0EU.
The Wildlife Trusts (Headquarters of County Wildlife Trusts), The Green,
    Witham Park, Waterside, Lincoln LN5 7JR.

Wildlife Food Suppliers

C. J. Wildbird Foods Ltd., The Rea, Upton Magna, Shrewsbury SY4 4UB.
Ernest Charles & Co. Ltd., Crediton, Devon EX17 2YZ
John E. Haith, Park Street, Cleethorpes, N.E. Lincolnshire DN35 7NF.
Garden Bird Supplies Ltd., Wem, Shrewsbury SY4 5BF.

Useful Addresses: North America

Wildflower Seeds, Bulbs & Plants

Albright Seed Company, 487 Dawson Drive #5S, Camarillo, CA 93012.
Bluestem Prairie Nursery, 13197 East 13th Road, Hillsboro, IL 62049.
Earthly Goods, Ltd., P.O. Box 614, New Albany, IN 47151.
Far West Bulb Farm, P.O. Box 515, Oregon House, CA 95962.
Fraser's Thimble Farm, 175 Arbutus Road, Salt Spring Island, BC, Canada V8K 1A3.
Great Basin Natives, P.O. Box 114, Holden, UT 84636.
Holland Wildflower Farm, P.O. Box 328, Elkins, AR 72727.
Homan Brothers Seed, P.O. Box 337, Glendale, AZ 85311.
Ion Exchange, 1878 Old Mission Drive, Harpers Ferry, IA 52146.
Landscape Alternatives, Inc., 1705 St. Albans Street, Roseville, MN 55113.
Larner Seeds, P.O. Box 407, Bolinas, CA 94924.
McClure & Zimmerman, P.O. Box 368, Friesland, WI 53935.
Moon Mountain Wildflowers, P.O. Box 725, Carpinteria, CA 93014.
NWN Nursery, 1365 Watford Circle, Chipley, FL 32428.
Native American Seed, 610 Main Street, Junction, TX 76849.
Native Gardens, 5737 Fisher Lane, Greenback, TN 37742.
Niche Gardens, 1111 Dawson Road, Chapel Hill, NC 27516.
Pacific Rim Native Plants, 44305 Old Orchard Road, Sardis, BC, Canada V2R 1A9.
Plants of the Southwest, Route 6, Box 11A, Agua Fria, Santa Fe, NM 87501.
Prairie Moon Nursery, Route 3, Box 163, Winona, MN 55987.
Prairie Nursery, P.O. Box 306, Westfield, WI 53964.
Robinett Bulb Farm, P.O. Box 1306, Sebastopol, CA 95473.
Stock Seed Farms, Inc., 28008 Mill Road, Murdock, NE 68407.
Sunlight Gardens, 174 Golden Lane, Andersonville, TN 37705.
Vermont Wildflower Farm, P.O. Box 5, Charlotte, VT 05445.
Western Native Seed, P.O. Box 1463, Salida, CO 81201.
Wild Earth Native Plant Nursery, 49 Mead Avenue, Freehold, NJ 07728.
Wild Seed, P.O. Box 27751, Tempe, AZ 85285.
Wildseed Farms, P.O. Box 3000, Fredericksburg, TX 78624.
Wildflowers from Nature's Way, 3162 Ray Street, Woodburn, IA 50275.

Native Trees

Stacy Adams Nursery, 1033 Jarrell Hogg Road, West Point, GA 31833.
Gardens of the Blue Ridge, P.O. Box 10, Pineola, NC 28662.
Mail-Order Natives, P.O. Box 9366, Lee, FL 32059.
Plants of the Wild, P.O. Box 866, Tekoa, WA 99033.
Woodlanders, Inc., 1128 Colleton Avenue, Aiken, SC 29801.

Conservation Organisations

Canadian Wildflower Society, Unit 12A, Box 228, Markham, ON, Canada L3R 1N1.
National Wildflower Research Center, 4201 La Crosse Boulevard, Austin, TX 78739.
New England Wild Flower Society, 180 Hemenway Road, Framingham, MA 01701.
North American Butterfly Association, 4 Delaware Road, Morristown, NJ 07960.
Theodore Payne Foundation for Wildflowers and Native Plants, 10459 Tuxford Street, Sun Valley, CA 91352.
Wild Ones—Natural Landscapers, P.O. Box 23576, Milwaukee, WI 53223.

❧ Appendix 5 ❧

Note on the Use of Imported Wildflower Seeds

In Britain, the majority of wildflower seeds used to create new wild-flower grasslands are sourced from continental Europe. Whilst this approach has been undertaken by many ecological restoration schemes, including many receiving financial support from their government or charities, concern is mounting about the use of exotic genestocks, particularly in Nature Reserves, Environmentally Sensitive Areas, and the like.

Flora Locale, whose principal aim is to protect indigenous wild plants and plant communities from introduced species and varieties, identify the potential dangers associated with this to include:

- erosion of native genestock through hybridization and genetic pollution;
- invasive aliens outcompeting the local species/landraces;
- consequences for the associated fauna and long-term survival of local plants due to differences in morphology and/or phenology of aliens; economic consequences due to scheme failures;
- 'imported' habitat not representing (and possibly not resembling) native vegetation characteristics.

They also offer in-depth guidelines for sourcing seed and plants (see below). In general, the collection of seeds and plants should only be undertaken for the purpose of establishing stock plants, and such collection and harvesting must avoid damage to the native plant and animal communities and work within the UK Wildlife and Countryside Act and Theft Act.

The publishers strongly recommend that anyone who is considering establishing a wildflower meadow should consult Flora Locale's Draft Technical Guidance Notes, available by email:

(floralocal@naturebureau.co.uk), or on their web site at:

http://www.naturebureau.co.uk/pages/floraloc/floraloc.htm

or by post from Flora Locale (see Useful Addresses: Britain).

The following publications, listed in the Bibliography, are also likely to be very helpful in this respect: *The Seed Savers Handbook* by Cherfas and Fenton; *Pastures New: How to create and care for wildflower meadows*, available from The Wildlife Trusts; *Lowland Grassland Management Handbook*, available from The Wildlife Trusts & English Nature; and *Wildflowers Work*, available from Landlife.

Bibliography

I have been an avid reader of wildlife books all my life, and certainly could not have written this book without reference to many of those mentioned below. I am most grateful to all their authors, and would recommend them to anyone wishing to read further on the subject of meadows and their wildlife. On the following page there is an additional list of relevant books published in North America.

Aichele D. & R., Schwegler H. W. & A.: *Wild Flowers of Britain & Europe*. Hamlyn, 1992.

Arnold E.N., Burton J.A. & Overenden D.W.: *A Field Guide to the Reptiles and Amphibians of Britain & Europe*. Collins, 1978.

Baines, Chris: *How to Make a Wildlife Garden*. Elm Tree Books,1985.

Baines, Chris & Smart, Jane: *A Guide to Habitat Creation*. Packard, 1991.

Bellamy, David: *Discovering the Countryside with David Bellamy: Grassland Walks*. Newnes Books, 1983.

Blamey, Marjorie & Fitter, Richard: *Wild Flowers of Britain & Northern Europe*. Diamond Books, 1994.

Burton, John A.: *Field Guide to the Mammals of Britain & Europe*. Kingfisher Books, 1991.

Cherfas, J. & Fenton, M.& J.: *The Seed Savers Handbook*. Grover Books, 1996.

Feltwell, John: *A Guide to Countryside Conservation*. Ward Lock, 1989.

Feltwell, John: *Meadows: A History and Natural History*. Alan Sutton, 1992.

Fitter, Alistair: *An Atlas of the Wild Flowers of Britain & Northern Europe*. Collins, 1978.

Fitter, R. & A., and Farrer, Ann: *Collins Guide to the Grasses, Sedges, Rushes & Ferns of Britain & Northern Europe*. Collins, 1983.

Gibbons, Bob & Liz: *Creating a Wildlife Garden*. Hamlyn, 1988.

Heinsel, H., Fitter, R. & Parslow, J.: *The Birds of Britain & Europe*. Collins, 1972.

Hofmann, Helga:*Wild Animals of Britain & Europe*. Harper Collins, 1995.

Hubbard, C.E.: *Grasses*. Third edition. Penguin, 1984.

Lowland Grassland Management Handbook. Wildlife Trusts/English Nature, 1994 (2nd edition due July 1998).

Mitchell, Alan: *A Field Guide to the Trees of Britain & Northern Europe*. Collins, 1988.

Pastures New: How to create and care for wildflower meadows. Wildlife Trusts, 1994.

Phillips, Roger: *Native & Common Trees.* Elm Tree Books, 1986.

Polunin, Oleg: *Flowers of Europe: A Field Guide.* Oxford University Press, 1969.

Rose, Francis: *The Wild Flower Key: British Isles - N.W. Europe.* Warne, 1981.

Stastny, Karel: *Birds of Britain & Europe.* Hamlyn, 1990.

Sterry, Paul: *Fungi of Britain & Northern Europe.* Hamlyn, 1991.

Sutton, D. & Bonson, R.: *Kingfisher Guide to Trees of Britain & Europe.* Kingfisher, 1990.

Thomas, E. & White, J.T.: *Hedgerow.* Dorling Kindersley, 1982.

Wildflowers Work. Landlife, National Wildflower Centre, 1997.

Wilkinson, J. & Tweedie, M.: *A Handguide to the Butterflies and Moths of Britain and Europe.* Treasure Press, 1986.

Zahradnik, J. & Severa, F.: *The Illustrated Book of Insects.* Treasure Press, 1991.

North American References

Art, Henry W.: *A Garden of Wildflowers.* Storey, 1986.

Ashworth, Suzanne: *Seed to Seed.* Seed Savers Exchange, 1991.

Beaubaire, Nancy, ed.: *Native Perennials.* Brooklyn Botanic Garden, 1996.

Burrell, C. Colston: *A Gardener's Encyclopedia of Wildflowers.* Rodale, 1997.

Daniels, Stevie: *The Wild Lawn Handbook.* Macmillan, 1995.

Druse, Ken, with Margaret Roach: *The Natural Habitat Garden.* Clarkson N. Potter, 1994.

Kress, Stephen W. *The Bird Garden.* Dorling Kindersley, 1995.

Lewis, Alcinda, ed.: *Butterfly Gardens.* Brooklyn Botanic Garden, 1995.

Loewer, Peter: *Step-by-Step Wildflowers & Native Plants.* Better Homes and Gardens Books, 1995.

Martin, Laura C.: *The Wildflower Meadow Book.* Globe Pequot, 1990.

Ottesen, Carole: *The Native Plant Primer.* Harmony Books, 1995.

Roth, Sally: *Natural Landscaping.* Rodale, 1997.

Scott, James A.: *The Butterflies of North America.* Stanford University Press, 1986.

Seidenberg, Charlotte. *The Wildlife Garden: Planning Backyard Habitats.* University of Mississippi Press, 1995.

Stevenson, Violet: *The Wild Garden.* Penguin, 1996.

Taylor, Patricia: *Easy-Care Native Plants.* Henry Holt, 1996.

Tekulsky, Matthew: *The Butterfly Garden.* Harvard Common Press, 1985.

Tufts, Craig, and Peter Loewer: *The National Wildlife Federation's Guide to Gardening for Wildlife.* Rodale, 1995.

Xerces Society: *Butterfly Gardening.* Sierra Club Books, 1990.

Index